THE
PRESENCE
INNER WORK

Cultivating a Deeper Connection with Self through Mindfulness, Meditation, and Spiritual Growth

DIEGO SIMON

THE PRESENCE INNER WORK
Cultivating a Deeper Connection with Self through Mindfulness, Meditation, and Spiritual Growth

Published by Diego Simon in 2024
www.presenceinnerwork.com

All rights reserved. No part of this book may be reproduced, copied, distributed or adapted in any form or by any means, electronic, mechanical, photocopying, recording or otherwise, with the exception of certain activities permitted by applicable copyright laws, such as brief quotations in the context of a review or academic work.

For permission to publish, distribute or otherwise reproduce this work, please contact the author at support@presenceinnerwork.com.

Copyright © Diego Simon, 2024

Diego Simon has asserted his right to be identified as the author of this work.

ISBN: 979-8-9899323-0-6
Ebook: 979-8-9899323-1-3

CONTENTS

Introduction 5

Chapter 1: The Demands of the Ego 22
    The Journey of Identity 29
    Contemplation and the Cosmic Presence 31
    Beyond the Demands of the Ego 36
    Deciphering the Ego 38

Chapter 2: The Silent Intelligence of the Being 42
    Flowing Close to the Being in Mindfulness 50
    Contemplation - The Mental Witness 52
    Contemplation During Physical Exercise 53

Chapter 3: Consonance with Nature - Rebuilding
    our Link with the Presence 56
    Contemplation - Embracing Reality without Labels 61
    The Mind and its Link with Existence 69

Chapter 4: Empowering Your Inner Being - Strengthening
    the Being in Everyday Life. 75
    The Pathways towards Pure Aspiration and Surrender 82
    Existence in Pure Consciousness 85
    The Instrument of the Divine Mother 88

Chapter 5: The Path Towards the Awakened Being 92
The Inner Witnessing Mind 94
The Awakening of the Inner Being 96
Emerging in the Divine Consciousness 99

Chapter 6: The Orchestrator of Emotional Reality 107
Unravelling the Dramatic Perception. 109
Challenging the Determination of the Unconscious 115
The Attitude of the Witness - Detachment in daily life 118
Surrender and Aspiration to the Will of the
Divine Being 120
Being Attached to the Mother of Consciousness 122

Chapter 7: The Shift of the Subjective Mind - From the Unaware Self to the Awakened Being 126
Contemplation-Unveiling the Subtlety of the Being 133
The Presence Discovers the Divine spark. 138
The Awakened Being brought to the Front. 142

Chapter 8: Reality in Consonance with Being 149
The Harmony of Being. 154
The Link with the Subtle Plane of Consciousness 159
Embracing the Reality of Consciousness 161

Chapter 9: Collective Memory - Transcending the Social Identity 168
Witness Consciousness 173
Beyond Collective Identity 176

INTRODUCTION

I would like to tell you briefly how my spiritual journey started. I want to share with you this experience as proof that spiritual life is not in conflict with working life or with daily adversities and challenges. Rather, the array of trials and tribulations, adversity, and antagonism can provide an opportunity for the being that resides beyond our mind, which contributes to unseating the notion of our "self."

My life as an entrepreneur in the textile industry, as co-owner of a business I ran with my brother, was marked by the constant need to face numerous adversities and setbacks, which I dealt with responsibly.

These circumstances, which at the time seemed to be obstacles, turned out to be the ideal conditions for a part of myself to open up and assimilate the teachings of an enlightened spiritual master, now deceased, who is noted as one of the main figures of mysticism in India.

With the perspective of time, I am deeply grateful for each timely event which, I now see, served the purpose of preparing the conditions in my psychology and mind for me to experience a spiritual awakening through deep meditation.

At about the age of 30, I found myself at the helm of the company I had co-founded with my brother, a business to which I had dedicated not only my time, but my life and dreams for fifteen years. At the time, the company was going through one of the worst crises in its history, with imminent risk of closure.

The future of this factory, on which we had staked our lives, was becoming clearer with each passing day. As the co-founder, I was completely dedicated, body and soul, to improving the company in which all the family savings were invested.

We entered into a hasty partnership with a friend from our youth, dazzled by the illusion of making our debut with the sale of laundry detergent to a giant retail chain in our country. Overnight, we embarked on a new business venture, transforming ourselves into a laundry detergent producer and supplier.

We won the coveted contract to supply the retail chain giant and, thanks to financial backing in the form of bank loans, and with the technical advice of suppliers and specialists, we were able to have the inventory ready to be distributed to hundreds of stores.

However, what initially promised to be a very lucrative new business turned out to be a complete disaster. After a few months, we were overwhelmed by the expenses, and were forced to withdraw our products from the stores.

Our hasty foray into the detergent business had significant repercussions. Over the next few years, our small textiles mill had to redouble its efforts to pay off the debt we had accumulated with the banks. It was necessary to keep production at maximum capacity and ensure everything was sold out so we could meet payments on time. This was the only way to pay off all the debt.

It took a few years before I realized that it was this discouraging scenario that put me on the path to rediscovering my authenticity—to return to the yearnings and aspirations in equality and fraternity among people who had been the main attraction in my life since my youth. I wanted to rebuild my life and live in community, according to my ideals, and for the two-week paid vacation I received that year from the company, I traveled to a community in southern India.

This trip was not intended to take me into any spiritual practice, but rather to participate in a lifestyle based on fraternity and harmony within the environment of a community of people coming from many parts of the world. In this wonderful community, I encountered, through their books, the spiritual teachings of a couple of enlightened masters, who were no longer physically present.

Such was my interest, and my affinity with the teachings from the books of these enlightened sages that, on returning to my country, I was absorbed in reading and assimilating their teachings in a practical way, and I was initiated into deep meditation.

I remember when, 17 years ago, during a quiet weekend afternoon, I experienced a deep meditation that transformed my perception. On that occasion, my attention was, as never before, prolonged in perfect silence. It was focused inside my body, in the center of my chest, at the level of my heart.

After that prolonged immersion, I experienced a complete surrender, feeling how my mind, in a perfect silence, penetrated a space of authentic peace. It was as if, by entering my own inner being—without the slightest interference of my mind—I had accessed a subtle space, where a pure love was born and self-sustained.

I experienced complete surrender, feeling how my mind, in silence, was immersed in a space of authentic peace. In that moment, a pure love emerged, a surrender and submission to the Will of the Divine Being.

While I was experiencing this pure love, and the attention of the witness part of the mind was submerged in a prolonged silence in the subtlety of my inner being, there arose in the center of my chest, inside my body, what was then only a tiny spark-like light. The notion of my person had been gradually giving way, reaching the point where it blurred. At that moment, my whole reality was the immersion in that subtlety, which was full of love and existence, from which this tiny spark had emerged.

Suddenly, the spark expanded, encompassing and absorbing the totality of the being. In that instant, my reality—my entire existence—became a being of wise energy shining, liberating, and flowing inside my thorax.

I felt how the wise energy flowed radiantly and liberatingly within my body, inside my thorax and head with an unimaginable rejuvenating effect that extended above my head. My whole life, at that moment, was summed up in the subtlety of that being of consciousness, which I experienced as the purest love: the most concrete, the most tangible, the most authentic, the most truthful, the most reliable, the most overflowing existence, and all without the slightest trace of a mind.

Everything about me was irrelevant, even my body. It was only when I felt the jolt caused by the flow of the wise cosmic energy of consciousness that the notion that I was present in that body, which was still trembling in parts, returned. The radiant sage energy continued to flow; it had penetrated my body, and made it vibrate with a new luster.

I had experienced being a part of existence in the purest, most overflowing, comforting, and trustworthy love. In my own flesh, I had become a being brimming with cosmic consciousness. I could never have imagined that the being could have such a full, real, truthful, blissful, and loving existence, as simply the subtlety of a wise cosmic consciousness, which encompassed my rib cage and the inside of my head.

In the same place where I used to return from work, feeling sometimes inconsolable because of the uncertainty in my business, something extraordinary happened when I entered the state of Samadhi, surrendering myself completely to the Divine Will. It was the most transforming, truthful, and forceful experience of spiritual awakening.

I remember feeling a deep gratitude to the Divine Mother, who took my surrendered being to bring it to the origin of its existence in one of the planes of consciousness in which she dwells.

That evening, as I walked to a store to buy groceries, my body felt rejuvenated. My step was light and the certainty of having experienced, just a short time prior, the existence of the being in the wise cosmic consciousness, in the purest love, predominated.

At that time, I did not know that this occurrence would be the beginning of a series of spiritual experiences. This led me to have a very active spiritual life in parallel to the person who played a leading role in the drama of my daily life, which was marked by the very delicate situation of the company.

During my deep meditation sessions, which I performed in the mornings or when I returned home from work, I felt certain that what the Divine Mother had designed for my spiritual progress would occur.

Early in the mornings or in the evenings, when I would return home after having dealt with yet another episode of business drama, I would immerse myself in deep meditation, guided by the consciousness of my enlightened masters. The being inside my body, would re-establish its existence in the inexhaustible source of consciousness it had repeatedly accessed.

The being had found its own formula to achieve the blurring of the "self": submissively surrendering in the truest aspiration for the Divine Will to be done, whether through the consciousness of my enlightened teachers or the Will of the Divine Mother. And once our mind finds the wise and refined posture to surrender and submit, in perfect silence and stillness, to the Will of the Divine Mother, the life of the spiritual practitioner is rewarded with a succession of experiences that have a profound transformative power in the being.

When I set out to meditate, I had no such thing as a desire or goal in mind. The routine was to submit myself in the most authentic surrender, so the Will of the Divine Mother would be done. During these moments, I would immerse myself in the perception of the presence, focusing on the inside of my body, on the place where the Divine spark had previously revealed itself.

I had become accustomed to entering the Samadhi of the awakened being, surrendered to the Will of my enlightened master's consciousness, in the intense spiritual practice I had been engaged in, all while experiencing complete uncertainty in my business life.

Simultaneously, my being experienced two things: a profound transformation, due to the frequency with which I was guided by the Divine Mother, impregnated with her grace, peace, and ecstasy, and also the drama of daily life, where I was pushed to the limit, overwhelmed by the ups and downs. The drama of daily life and my spirituality resembled the piston of an engine: first driven to the bottom in the midst of trials and tribulations and then experiencing an explosion of certainty, a fulfilled value, and transformation. Progress on the level of consciousness was occurring at full speed.

Even amid the storm the company was going through, with the latent risk of closure, there was one person who remained optimistic and comforted. I had found the being that influenced my daily perspective and could give the correct value to what was happening.

The challenge was to maintain a being ready to emerge in its Samadhi, surrendered to the Will of my enlightened master, while facing the daily plight of the company. This meant that, during the meditation sessions, the being was completely detached from its leading role in the work environment and was ready to enter into attunement with the consciousness of the spiritual master.

Thus, my spiritual life and the transformative process that was taking place in the being only reaffirmed my spiritual conviction in the progress of the being and strengthened me in the face of the worst challenges and uncertainties.

Over the course of three years, during which I experienced the spiritual awakening and the blessings of the experiences that followed in deep meditation, I found myself engaged in my work life, supported by a solid team of collaborators as I faced the business crisis.

During those years, I witnessed a profound transformation with regards to the awakened being, led on several occasions to imbibe the higher planes of consciousness under the guidance of the consciousness of my enlightened master. And it took this long for me to obtain a moderate sum of money that was enough to allow my longing to return to India to dedicate myself to the spiritual life to come to pass.

Once I had fulfilled my promise to deliver a new machine that would double production and allow the company to face the debts to the banks with greater security, I was ready to embark on a new stage of my life as a spiritual practitioner.

I've never felt more at home than in India. I experienced a unique connection to its environment, which was perfect for the being. Spirituality permeated the atmosphere, whether in the ashram or in the company of my devoted spiritual practitioner colleagues. The aura of consciousness of the enlightened masters, who during their lifetime did the spiritual work of opening paths to higher planes, contributed to the ideal environment for spiritual practice.

Introduction

During the six months of my stay in India, almost without exception, I meditated every day at the shrine, where the relics of my two enlightened masters rest in their mausoleum.

In the midst of a pristine spiritual atmosphere, in deep meditation, the awakened being repeatedly entered into the state of Samadhi and, already completely surrendered to the Will of the Divine Being through the consciousness of my enlightened master, a series of spiritual experiences took place—experiences I shared with both young and veteran spiritual practitioners, including those who were already benefitting from spiritual realization.

This was the start of my spiritual journey, and it can be yours as well. Remember that spiritual life flourishes amid daily struggles, illuminating a path of transformation and authenticity.

In this book, spiritual practice is approached in an integral way, showing how it is inseparable from your daily life. In each chapter, we explore the functioning of the mind at the level of consciousness—with an experiential approach. This approach is ready to be incorporated in a practical way, adapting to the originality and uniqueness of your individual perspective, as well as to the circumstances of your life.

In life, it is our own existence that guides our being through a formative process, leading us toward the transcendence of our "self." This life reveals itself as the stage where we all contribute to forging the conditions that will propitiate a tangible encounter between the aspects of the presence and the inner being, which are fundamental components of our mind. Although inadvertently, the roles we play in society contribute significantly to this process of transcendence that is gestated at the level of consciousness, within our own mind.

Until now, in the experiences we have on a daily basis, through the concept of our "self" that was generated by the subjective mind, the being is "embedded" in a process of development. Although this process is not always the most efficient, it is maturing so that at some point in time, the conditions are given to allow the union of its original components: the presence and the spark of the Divine in the inner being.

Can we be humble enough to accept a new relationship with reality in the present? Can we allow our identity to not be defined by the character that plays a role in society? What lies beyond the constant little voice that resides in our minds? How can we free ourselves from the tyranny of the mind and let the present moment be as it is?

I want to share with you the different scenarios where the interaction of the mind is revealed in this process, as the being moves forward to emancipate itself from the notion of "self" and, in this way, restore its reality in consciousness. I want to present you with concise information, sufficient for you to acquire the knowledge and practical methodology necessary to undertake a spiritual practice with a view to spiritual awakening. In short, this book is a guide to a deeper understanding of yourself and the spiritual journey you are destined to undertake.

Introduction

This book is designed to resonate with you in that process that goes unnoticed, but which is constantly unfolding at the level of the consciousness of your being.

Here you will find recurring words and expressions, sometimes in excess, but with the intention of immersing yourself in the process that occurs behind the mind, beyond the notion of your person. The lines of this text emerge from the deepest part of the being and seek to connect with your mind, identifying the addressee in the very being you carry within you.

It is a guide, molded in words, that comes from the same level of consciousness you harbor. Its mission is to transcend the concept of your person. The part which ultimately assimilates this wisdom is the part of you that already carries enough receptivity and sensitivity to adopt these teachings in a practical way.

In the new generation of spiritual seekers and practitioners, we see the influence of their being leading them to break free from the dependence on which they held their value, esteem, and sense of belonging on roles, expectations, and values rooted in the idiosyncrasies of the collective.

Not only has there been an increase in the adoption of purifying practices in people's daily lives, but the influence of the self that goes beyond the mind, with the purpose of transcending the concept of "self" and immersing oneself in the reality of consciousness, has also gained momentum.

In today's lifestyle, we observe the abandonment of ideas, customs, values, and expectations that are based on the idiosyncrasy of the collective. A new generation emerges that opts for a simple life, aligned with its authenticity, independent of the idiosyncrasies of the collective. At the same time, they abandon the consumerist ideas and habits in which the masses participate.

This reflection of the transformation process, driven by the progress of the self at the level of consciousness, exerts its influence to remove obstacles that hinder the stride toward transcendence. The being finds an ally in a simpler, humbler, and more authentic version of our person that cooperates in the process, unbeknownst to us, at the level of consciousness to decipher the notion of our "self."

The being, as an inseparable part of our mind, does not have to deal with the concept of "self" that depends heavily on sustaining its value, esteem, and sense of security in the ideas, customs, expectations, values, and feelings of the collective.

What is even more important is that this new generation, because of its independence, lives its day-to-day life, its reality, and its present practically without sharing the ideas of the idiosyncrasy or involving its feelings in the temperament of the collective. The present of these people no longer follows the vertiginous rhythm in which the person seeks their value and esteem in what the idiosyncrasy recognizes and values, diminishing the speculative activity. The activity of the mind—which generates images to replace the instant in the here and now, in the present, making judgments, supposing, conjecturing, predicting, suspecting, and involving their feelings—is reduced.

In the minds of these people, the distance to the consciousness of the being has been shortened. Just as more and more individuals are breaking away from old structures in which the collective consciousness functions, this indicates that the spirit is emancipating itself from what hinders it in the progress that leads to transcending the concept of the "self," previously sustained in the idiosyncrasies of the collective. This book is an invitation to explore this spiritual journey and to discover the authenticity that resides in your own being.

Our individual perspectives are shaped by the collective reality. If we do not strive to purify our perception, we will continue to be influenced by the collective environment in our intellectual and emotional views and experiences.

This book leads us to embrace the simplicity and authenticity of the presence, understanding that it is not necessary to seek external purposes or meanings to experience it. The presence is revealed through silent attention, in serenity and stillness.

This path is not to deny the conceptual mind, but to balance it with the wisdom of the inner being. It is to recognize that intelligence goes beyond analysis and judgment, that it resides in mindfulness and connection with wholeness.

This work guides you through life from this transparent identity, feeling the echo of consciousness in every step you take, in every interaction you have. In this state, you are an active participant in the dance of existence, and the co-creator of moments that are full of meaning and beauty.

By embracing your transparent identity, you will allow yourself to be more than just ego limitations and conceptual labels. You will become a being in harmony with the whole, a conscious co-creator in this cosmic dance.

In this union of the mind and the being, in this transparent and spontaneous identity, you will discover a new way of going about life: a dance in which each movement is an expression of your connection with the presence, a unique melody in the symphony of existence.

As we continue our inner journey, we understand that the presence is a constant component in our mind, always available to bring us to a state of equanimity and deeper perception. The Presence, in its pure state, is the key to an existence in harmony, peace, grace and beauty; and it is available to all of us through silent attention.

Throughout the following pages, you will learn that by penetrating into the presence's perception in your mind can unleash the liberation of the ingrained idea of "self," which was molded by the idiosyncrasies of the collective. This simple act will open before you new perspectives and dimensions in the understanding of your being.

We will move toward the recognition of a being that is separate from your physical body and the complex social implications that surround it. The liberated part of you, connected to your wise presence, will unveil unexplored layers of knowledge about your true nature.

As you delve deeper into this inner journey, you will discover that this independent being exists beyond social definitions, including gender, race, sexual orientation, community membership, or social position.

By immersing yourself in contemplation, you will leave behind the meanings that shape your interpretations. Through this process, you will become adept at the inquiry and purification of your wise presence. Here, you will emerge into a new version of yourself.

As you advance in contemplative practice, you will experience the first glimmer of your presence. In that instant, you will recognize that your being in the here and now transcends the notion of "self" that was constructed based on social expectations. You will cease to construct a persona and you will embrace your authentic essence.

Now, connect with the cosmic essence that constantly flows within you, generating a sociocultural and worldly understanding. In your mind resides the reality of cosmic Presence, unfolding in its state of consciousness. However, the superficial soul charge tends to mask this cosmic existence with conceptual realities. In this link with the cosmic essence, you will find the key to transcending conceptual limitations and embracing the fullness of your presence. This experience is not merely conceptual; it is an intimate connection with the realm of consciousness. The cosmic Presence gives us unmediated understanding and transcends collective emotional influence.

By following the path outlined in the following pages, you will constantly practice observing your mind as an impartial witness. You will free your consciousness from the trap of the interpretative "self" and allow it to develop in its own nature, which will bring you closer to a deeper perception of your presence. Let us immerse ourselves in the direct experience of Cosmic Presence.

This path I offer you is an opportunity for transformation, of bringing your being into consciousness. In these pages, you will find what you need for the first stage of your spiritual journey. Various methods of purification are presented which, when assimilated and made part of your daily life, serve to bring forth the wise presence of mind.

This book is more than words on pages; it is an invitation to live consciously, to embrace the totality of your being and to participate fully in the symphony of existence. If you follow the path laid out and you practice the unbiased observation of your mind, then you will pave the way to a deeper perception of your presence. This is just the beginning of your spiritual journey.

It is your wise presence that will bring about the transformation that is necessary to blur the notion of "self." The daily experience, seen from this renewed perspective, will contribute to clarify and remove obstacles on your path towards the transcendence of the notion of "self" at the level of your consciousness.

Through this experience, I want to demonstrate to you that you possess all that is necessary to reveal the Divine spark that resides inside your physical body, in the being of consciousness that dwells within you. At this very moment, everything is ready for you to channel it, cooperating with the design of establishing its existence at the origin of your consciousness.

By allowing even a hint of the perspective of the presence to emerge, the influence of the being takes prominence in our life, which accelerates the process in which our mind acquires the conditions in which deep meditation will unveil the spark of the Divine you carry within your inner subtle body.

Purification is of the utmost importance for the spiritual aspirant, as it allows the nature of their consciousness to prevail in contemplation and in the meditation sessions.

All of this will contribute to the emergence of the wise presence of mind. And it is this wise presence, in its stillness and silence, along with the other aspects that it possesses by its nature in consciousness, where you will discover the master of spiritual practice within yourself.

CHAPTER 1

The Demands of the Ego

On the path to transcending the notion of "self," we enter into the subjective activity of the mind that supplants the original consciousness of our being. The part of your mind that aligns itself with the emancipated, self-sufficient, independent existence of the consciousness of your being does not need to rely on concepts to interact with the present reality. This authentic identity of your being, in its spontaneity and innocence, avoids categorizing and judging, allowing itself to witness the environment without rushing to exert influence. It is exposed, open, accepting the flow of the instant in the here and now, without disturbing its state of serenity, restlessness, and silence.

This connection with existence in the present moment, in the here and now, is characterized by the absence of the creation of the distinction of "self." In this state, there is no "self" exerting its influence by bringing in concepts or views, or making use of accumulated understanding. Instead, there is a part in our mind that synchronizes with our presence, accepting without interference the flow of the present moment completely free of meanings, concepts or notions.

In our purifying practice, our mind needs us to give it opportunities to be in environments where the experience it stores in its conscious memory practically falls into disuse. A space where there is almost no need to engage in interpretive activity, which gives it meaning based on accumulated understanding—however minimal—thus creating a pause in this constant flow of thoughts.

We purify our mind by getting it used to coming into alignment with this emancipated, self-sufficient part of it that is not sustained by meanings or concepts. This process occurs because, by allowing it to resonate with the state of its component of consciousness, the mind acquires and becomes imbued with the reality of its presence. In this deep connection, the mind is freed from the bondage of interpretations and immersed in the authenticity of its consciousness.

In your mind, the original consciousness of your being conducts a unique process. Your being deciphers the notion of "self" to reestablish its conscious reality in your mind. The mind undertakes a unique and very particular path, because your being seeks to transcend that individual pattern of emotional intelligence, vital energy, and subconsciousness that is the notion of our "self." The combination of the intelligent-emotional, vital, and subconscious facets creates a unique pattern of configuration of consciousness (with which the being in our own mind interacts to transcend it). For the consciousness of our being to transcend this subjective functioning, it is necessary for the mind to cease to identify itself with the roles, archetypes, style referents, and manners with which it reinforces its inclusion, sense of security, and belonging in the collective.

The mind must free itself from generating this notion based on models and stereotypes, in order to allow expansion into a liberating authenticity.

Let's continue with an in-depth analysis of how our mind operates in interaction with our environment and with others. Let's see how the activity of the realm of emotional intelligence and its record in our mind influences the way we relate to the world.

The process of generating an image of how we are perceived by others is a clear example of how our mind elaborates on and brings to the surface information stored in memory. As we explore this process of constructing the notion of the "self," it becomes clear how this subjective elaboration unfolds. By bringing the subjective activity of the mind into the open, we give the wisdom of our witness consciousness a tool so that, in its detachment, it can approach the authenticity and fullness of its true self.

When acting in a situation with a group of people, the mind focuses on what is happening in that moment, but at the same time, the memory is recognizing and interpreting the information according to the idiosyncratic meanings of its past experience.

Are you familiar with the sensation of interpreting how others perceive you? At some point, when we are interacting with other people, we have a concept of how they perceive us. In that moment, we're speculating, bringing about a series of images of how others perceive us. We're applying meanings from the idiosyncratic understanding of our past experience.

Our mind is elaborating on a series of images, stemming from its sociocultural or idiosyncratic experience that is accumulated in our memory. Since the experience we have accumulated in our memory has been recorded from the realm of emotional intelligence, we transform the reality in our mind to the present moment in that same format of configuration of consciousness.

This is the subjective functioning of the mind. The mind doesn't even need to narrate what is happening with an internal voice. Emotion is faster, and our point of view comes in the form of an image. That is the notion we have of our person in that moment.

The truth is that the view we have of how other people perceive us may be very close to what they are thinking, because we share the same idiosyncrasies. How seriously do we take idiosyncrasy? How much does our own sense of value depend on it? How much is our emotional disposition involved? The answers to these questions vary from person to person.

But the truth is that people living in a community share a set of values, expectations—and temperament. We—and the people we interact with—generate the images of our expectations from the accumulated experience we have learned from the idiosyncrasy of the collective.

We see ourselves in a series of situations in which we acquire status and feel worthy of value in the eyes of others.

But what is it that tells us the value and the role we play in the scenario or context that we create in our mind?

In the same way that, at home, there is a set of agreements in which we live together as a family, in society, people participate in a set of consensuses, expectations, customs, values, and in the temperament of the collective.

Beginning in childhood, we learn to construct the idea of our "self," according to the values, customs, and expectations of our family and our closest community. And as we grow up, not only do these roles change, but the concepts of value—in which we involve our soul disposition, our emotional part—multiply.

We construct the notion of our "self" in roles and conventions that we act out according to the idiosyncrasy of the collective in which we have been conditioned with our sense of value and self-esteem.

We grade our past performances. We interpret and judge whether or not the condition or situation in the moment meets our expectations.

We anticipate what is going to happen, in order to maintain our value and esteem.

While we are engaged in our thoughts, we not only rate them according to value, but we also involve our emotional disposition. Our emotions are implicit in the images we create of what has already happened, of what we interpret as happening at the moment, or in the prediction we make of what is about to happen.

The conceptual images we develop are related to the sense of what is or is not acceptable, beneficial, or valuable—both for us and for the group of people we are with. They are related to what brings a sense of satisfaction, enjoyment, and joy because it strengthens and consolidates. Or what brings emotions of fear, anxiety, vulnerability, or resentment, because it affects, alters, or invalidates our conception of order, security, trust, inclusion, belonging, or goodwill among others.

Likewise, when we are in the middle of a conversation, our mind—and those of the interlocutors—pays attention to recognize the meanings of the realm of emotional intelligence that is recorded in our conscious memory.

In the middle of a conversation, our mind uses its attention and intelligence to understand what is being talked about, and in turn transits through the accumulated understanding of our past experiences to bring forth ideas or elaborate points of view, with which it contributes to the conversation.

What we hear produces images or concepts of the intelligent facets that are accompanied, albeit imperceptibly, by an emotional charge or a state of mind.

The experience to which the mind has recourse in its memory is not only conceptual or rational content but is always accompanied by a certain degree of our emotions.

While the "self" seeks to reestablish its value, it also engages its emotions. There is an emotional response to one degree or another.

We engage our emotions in states of mind. They range from tranquility to anxiety, from enjoyment to nervousness, from contentment and optimism to fear and trepidation, from satisfaction to dissatisfaction, and from vulnerability to resentment, just to mention a few.

The search for value encompasses a large part of our mind's activity.

The consciousness of our being is taken up in the speculative activity of the "self" that seeks to reestablish its value and esteem in every moment.

The perspective of the "self" ignores its consciousness of being and that, in its judgments, conjectures and assumptions, it is misaligned with the present, in the here and now of the presence.

The truth is that the search for value is an impulse very close to the authenticity of our being.

Value is what we feel as potentiality-for-being: to be wholly "myself"—the strength of existence.

The ability to feel free, talented, skillful, dexterous, confident, abundant, kind, empathetic, generous, creative, and original, among others.

We value what we believe gives us the capacity to exist.

Since we consider idiosyncratic reality as the sustenance of our value, we strongly embrace the roles, character models, forms, styles, and mannerisms we deem acceptable to our society.

However, from the ego's perspective, value enters into the intensity, the vehemence, and the reactivity of its needs, drives, and demands. To a large extent, the ego is a formation of the vital, so its motivation is the satisfaction, sometimes impulsive, of its desires and demands.

The impulses of the ego become a defining factor in our personality.

The ego's perspective seeks the notoriety, the spectacular, that which influences others with intensity. It longs to encompass its experience by expanding so that it is recognizable to others.

When we feel that we are the focus of attention, that is the moment of glory for our ego. Pridefulness puts the ego on its podium, on its pedestal, and we feel the strength of our "self."

So, in the vast space of our consciousness, we have discovered that we often forget the inner melody that guides us to authenticity. We instead dance to the rhythm of the expectations and roles that society imposes.

The Journey of Identity

Within the journey of introspection, on the way to the transcendence of the "self," we encounter a challenge that profoundly affects our relationship with the very essence of our being. This challenge lies in how the mind has lost its center—that place where the serenity and peace of inner presence converge. The ego, in its eagerness to define and project a limited notion of self, has distorted the true nature of our consciousness. As we move forward, we will see how this influence of the ego has been weaving a web that distances us from the essence of the true self, blocking channels of connection with its authenticity, reasonableness, and humility. This dynamic has led us to value ourselves through a constructed persona, seeking external validation and compromising our relationship with the authenticity of the being.

Now, let us delve into how our ego's influence has shaped our perception and how we can reclaim the true center of our existence.

Our mind had lost its central position—that center where we enter in consonance with serenity, calmness, and the peace of the presence.

The egoic entity has been making the presence and consciousness of the being the notion of our idiosyncratic and mundane "self." To continue means that the mind blocks the channels of the original consciousness of the self through the conditioning in which we value ourselves.

Our "self" had been using the consciousness of our being to create an identity that supports its worth, its esteem, its security, and its sense of belonging, thus seeking to please others and obtain their approval.

Recovering the mind's center involves recognizing the influence of the ego and then transcending it. As we immerse ourselves in the practice of self-inquiry and contemplation, we begin to unravel the threads of ego that have woven the fabric of our identity. With determination and tenacity, we can delve into the deep layers of consciousness and probe the ingrained beliefs that have shaped our perception of ourselves. We begin to free ourselves from the need for external validation and find a more genuine source of self-worth and acceptance. The process of returning to our mind's center is a path of authenticity and emancipation. We connect with the serenity and peace that reside in our being, allowing consciousness to regain its central position in our experience.

Ultimately, the loss of center, which is caused by the ego's influence, can be transformed into an opportunity for self-discovery and growth. It is a constant reminder of the importance of re-establishing clarity, equanimity, and humility, where we come into alignment with the unchanging essence of our presence.

Consciousness, in its interaction with the notion of our person, is unique and individual. There is no other mind that experiences reality like yours. All the models, roles, and social forms of society, are like suits in which we dress up our mind.

By occupying our mind with following models, roles, styles, and forms, adopting them as if they are part of our reality, we add resistance to the obstacle that, at the level of consciousness, the inner being is trying to decipher in our mind.

The perspective from which we experience each day is ours alone. It corresponds to the configuration of consciousness and the way our mind records, recognizes, and interprets each moment.

The configuration of consciousness in our mind experiences each day as if it were a composer. We might share the same scenario with our family members, co-workers, and friends, but each of us creates and recreates a unique perspective of reality.

Can we be so humble as to accept a new relationship to existence in the here and now, other than that of the persona that presents itself in society?

Nature reminds us of humility: a cow, for example, roams without competing or seeking recognition.

Contemplation and the Cosmic Presence

When contemplating, what we do is observe, one by one, from the position of the witness, the points of view, thoughts, concepts, impressions, or any other subjective content of the mind, from the moment it arises until it fades away in its journey through our mind.

As we observe, one by one, the thoughts that pass through our mind, we realize that we are not those thoughts, but the being that remains in perfect stillness and silence as they pass by: imperturbable, immovable. We are in the witness part of the mind, which is the perception that is approaching our presence. By prolonging the stillness and silence, we observe the movement of our mind that seeks to bring meaning. We detach ourselves from each of the meanings with which our mind pretends to recognize this instant of stillness and silence. We thus remain in the position of the observer.

By maintaining the position of the witness, we perceive that the views, concepts, or thoughts that arise in our mind are part of a relative reality. If they were all of reality, we would not be able to observe ourselves from the immovable attention of the witness consciousness.

We are aware that the concepts that pass through our mind are not the ultimate reality. And what is more, we discover a more subtle reality in the spaces of alert attention that begin to open up.

The mind ceases interpreting the superficial reality of concepts and meanings, from the experience it has accumulated in its memory. That clear, subtle, and free perception of meaning that unfolds is our whole reality.

The conceptual perception of the mind that intrudes upon everything it has access to in its own thoughts or what it observes happening in the moment fades away.

A fissure is opening where our being exists in the consciousness of which it is made. That is its essence, the most natural form of its existence, because our mind has always been just consciousness.

The subjectivity of our mind ceases, and the concept of our identity is blurred; in its place, there is a very attentive, alert, and conscious perception, free of meaning. At that moment, that subtle plane of existence is our entire reality. We accept it completely, surrendering unconditionally, without waiting, and without trying to understand.

The functioning of our mind yields and gives way to the unified perception of our presence.

The Presence emerges in a state where there is no longer the notion of our "self." Instead, the mind is absorbed in the concentration of the Presence. We are experiencing a pure state of concentrated attention. It is simply the present, free of meaning, in the purest concentration of the consciousness. Really, it is concentration, because as the element of the presence emerges from our mind, attention is intensified in silence.

This is how cosmic Presence exists: where all reality is immersed. The contents of the mind, its thoughts, its concepts, its ideas, and its emotions are immersed in Presence.

The ability that our mind possesses to pay attention—the same one that is sometimes crowded or immersed in its thoughts—originates in the consciousness of the Presence.

The purest, most intense attention is the concentration of the Presence. Even if there is not yet a spiritual awakening, the presence that is one of the components of our mind's consciousness can emerge in its pure state. This is the concentration of consciousness. It is the reality in which the Presence exists in its pure state.

The path of purification leads us to a profound reconfiguration of our mind and perspective, marking a significant transition towards a more authentic and liberated identity. During this process, the mind sheds the meanings and chains that previously sustained the superficial notion of "self," disassociating itself from the search for external validation and identification with predefined roles. The re-emergence of our authentic presence reveals the incongruence that previously went unnoticed in our daily actions.

With an open heart and a clear mind, we leave behind the shadows of ego and embrace the sanity of being authentic.

In one fell swoop, the mind is stripped of a series of meanings that gave impetus to its subjective functioning. The mind ceases to identify itself with a series of notions that maintain a gap between itself and the consciousness of its being in its own mind.

We have purified our mind of the impulses of the ego. Its needs, demands, preferences, and convictions are simply a shadow of the clarity, transparency, and spontaneity of the person that resonates more with the true self.

Now, we realize when we're trying to evade the self-sufficiency and originality of our authentic self. We are aware of the part of ourselves that tries to remain sheltered in the ideas, customs, values, and expectations, sharing the feeling of the collective. We are more sensitive to the distortions and the resistance that arise when we try to evade the responsibility of our authentic "self": a more transparent, spontaneous, and innocent identity that transcends conventions.

We always knew there was a part in us that was above and beyond having to follow and take its value and esteem from the prescribed conventions of role or character modeling that we were exposed to from a very early age.

Maintaining the veil of a personality built on idiosyncrasy meant being on guard to act and exist according to the expectations of what confers value.

But now the mind can give up the value, the security, the sense of belonging that these meanings conferred on it. We can find our own means to feel valuable, secure, confident, useful, and productive.

We stop functioning in the old structures. We now resonate more with the nature of being in our mind, and a simplified way of looking at life arises from within us.

This new identity is aligned with what we feel is most authentic in our person. It is a step towards authenticity, emancipation, self-sufficiency, generosity, and detachment.

In the intimacy of our mind, the influence of the inner being begins to intensify. What happens on the surface in our day-to-day life contributes to the progress of the being that seeks to transcend the notion of our "self."

Now, the progress of our being no longer depends on participating in the pathology of the ego of the collective.

The instability and emotional involvement that our mind experienced when participating in the frenetic, ego-alienating rhythm of the collective becomes evident.

We leave the place reserved for us; the role prescribed by the idiosyncrasy of the collective. We no longer need it. Our development is already taking place at a different pace. Our feelings, desires, motivations, and intentions are becoming more and more aligned with purity, benevolence, and the frankness that originates in our being.

We are already under the influence of being. It is opening a new perspective for us, and it calls us to live in the natural rhythms of our being.

After immersing ourselves in contemplation and detachment from the mental activity in which the notion of "self" is generated, we resonate more with the being that goes unnoticed, but which dwells behind the mind. Just by having allowed a hint of perception to emanate in equanimity—in alert attention that passes in silence and free of meaning—our mind has been purified. It has been imbued with the consciousness component of presence. This presence, in its coexistence with our inner being, has tightened and intensified its synergy. It has accelerated the process in which the being has the objective of deciphering and transcending the notion of our person.

Beyond the Demands of the Ego

Behind the facade of "self," our being is exerting its influence to establish its priority in our life; underlying this is the subtle but profound influence of the inner being. This influence acts as a wise guardian that adjusts our direction. As this influence gains strength, we begin to discover incongruities in our previous roles and attitudes. By purifying the mind, we see life from a wiser and calmer perspective.

Consequently, the harmony of inner consciousness begins to shape the way we interact with the world, replacing the need for external validation with a deeper connection, one that is more in tune with our authentic essence.

Behind the notion of our "self," at the level of consciousness, the stillness and silence of a wise presence influence the mind to adopt, even if only partially, the aspects of its simplicity, humility, acceptance, equanimity, and mindfulness in the here and now.

Through contemplative practice, our mind has positioned itself more in the center: in its balance, in serenity, in simplicity, and in the here and now. It has learned to become more in tune with reality, in the here and now of the presence.

Facing the humility of accepting a fresh relationship with existence and moving away from the pre-established role of a persona in society challenges us to embrace simplicity and authenticity.

We are purifying the notion of a "self" that we have used to invest its talent and its capabilities in seeking approval, acceptance, and recognition from people who were seeking to satisfy their own ego-centric purposes.

The influence of the being within us is hidden, but incisive. Its influence acts as a wise guardian that repeatedly rectifies the trajectory of our life.

Increasing the influence of the being makes us see the incongruity when we pretend or act in roles that do not correspond to our true self.

We purify our mind and can see our life, who we are, our actions, and our motivations from a perspective that puts everything in its proper place.

In that person who sought at every moment to take advantage, to achieve results, to compete, to influence others and to feel important, we now see that there is a sensible, humble being who can remain calm, in a state of serenity.

The influence of this being keeps us aloof from what may identify us with the consumerist habits and lifestyles with which we could slow our progress, with a view to unseating the notion of our "self."

From the simple and clear perspective of this humble being, it is revealed that we were acting from the ego, which captured every moment—transforming it into something it could use to reaffirm its value, importance, and power to exert its influence.

With the practice of contemplation, our presence emerges more and more, thus removing from our being that which distances us from authenticity.

This transition has led us to perceive and understand life from a broader and truer perspective—one in which our authentic essence shines through more clearly.

Deciphering the Ego

As we advance on the path of consciousness, it becomes evident that our perspective has evolved, moving closer to the being. However, as we follow this path, we face the challenge of balancing the voice of the ego with the serene wisdom of the true self.

This natural progress is met with resistance from the ego, which clings to its dominance and seeks to hold captive the authentic and sensitive part of our person (it has accustomed us to respond according to its demands and impulses). The conflict between the being that yearns for detachment and exploration of the presence and the ego that seeks to stand out and compete creates a duality in our experience.

Our perspective comes from a "self" that has come closer to the consciousness of its being. In our mind, there is a part that has taken more of the verve, clarity, sensitivity, perception, and perspective of the being.

Now this part of the mind notices and rejects what it finds dissonant to its detachment, equanimity, humility, and sacrifice.

However, the progress of the being that occurs quite naturally at the level of consciousness encounters the ego, which is reluctant to relinquish its control.

The ego is unwilling to yield and intends to hold captive the part of our person that resonates with authenticity, reasonableness, and humility—and that is adept at the inquiring, enlightening, and renewing practice of the presence.

We live in the uncertainty and the contrariety created by the competition between the adherence to detachment, inquiry, intuition, enlightenment, the ally of the presence and its adversary, the ego that has been accustomed to distinguish itself, to show off, and become notorious.

The egoic part interprets our detachment, our letting go, our being more in the here and now, as if we are throwing our humanity overboard.

The perspective of the ego will try to persuade us that, by adopting the authentic, original, and our sensible identity, we are dispossessing ourselves of our value—of the confidence and security we have because of our virtues, talent and humanity. It deceives us by creating dramatic images to take us away from the simplicity and humility that brings us closer to the heart of our most genuine qualities. It reacts by manipulating our moods, making us feel fragile, vulnerable, and incomplete.

However, by embracing our authentic identity, we free ourselves from the need to sustain our value in predefined roles and models. Authenticity brings us into a space where our presence connects directly with the essential qualities of the being, stripped of masks and external conditioning.

By living the authentic and original version of ourselves, we no longer base our value, esteem, security, and confidence—nor our sense of belonging—on the roles, role models, conventions, and idiosyncrasies of society.

The transition from the inner struggle between authenticity and the influence of the ego leads us, through contemplative practice, to a space of reunion with the essence of the Presence.

When we set out to contemplate, we strip ourselves of the identity which sustains its value and esteem in what is understood in common agreement with the circle of people around us.

The meanings that maintain the idiosyncratic notion of our being are not compatible with the being that exists only as consciousness.

When we allow our wise presence to emerge, we can observe from its perspective the subjective activity of our mind.

The more our mind is in tune with the being, the more calm it will experience, the more balance, the more joy. There is an authentic enjoyment of life to be found here.

CHAPTER 2

The Silent Intelligence of the Being

How can we go through our daily activities feeling safe and without resorting to the conceptual interpretation that we carry out in each moment? We might feel vulnerable without the interpretative understanding that the mind habitually performs throughout the day.

In the journey of the mind, certain concepts have emerged as familiar havens—safe ground where comfort and understanding can be found. They are familiar islands that connect to the known, but they can also separate the mind from the richness of the present, from experiencing the presence in the here and now.

The mind, however, is known for not dwelling on mere categories or conceptual interpretations; it adds voice to its creations. We possess that inner voice, like a guide whispering in the corridors of our mind, signaling to us the things that require our attention. "Herein lies what is important," it tells us. "This deserves to be observed."

It is as if we substitute our true experience of the present moment with what the little voice tells us—as if the mind needs a signal to indicate what is interesting, what is significant, and what is relevant.

The little voice, the verbalized narration, only strengthens the notion that there is a person observing our surroundings.

The fact that our mind resorts to this little voice is completely understandable. Consider that, from a very early age, we have been recording, creating, and recreating the concept of our "self" and the world around us through the concepts of language that correspond to the emotional intelligence of our mind.

However, when the mind elaborates its representations through language, it reinforces the concept that our "self" is separate from our immersion in attention, in silence, and in harmony with the perception of our being.

Our mind is distracted from the immersion of its attention in the here and now. It anticipates a meaning, in order to recognize and interpret the reality in front of it. It elaborates concepts, points of view, and thoughts—which it uses to interpret reality in the moment. It is this distance that generates subjective functioning.

But there is another way to be in the moment and that is without the voice that functions as our guide, without the signal. And this is a big step in bringing the mind closer to its presence.

The reality is that we do not require the conceptual images we create with language and apply to our experiences in order to be intelligent. We carry intelligence within the consciousness component from which the mind is made. Intelligence is not necessarily analysis, judgment, reason, or speculative activity. It is also the full attention of the presence in harmony, inspiration, intuition, and vision. By thinking in silence, without developing a conceptual interpretation, we are disposing of our intuition—the intelligence that is intrinsic in the consciousness component of our mind.

Attention comes from the presence. Intuition and inspiration come from our inner being. Subjective functioning, which creates views, concepts, and thoughts, uses the medium of the consciousness of the being that is in the mind itself.

The intelligent component of consciousness is the one that takes the form of the concepts with which we interpret, value, classify, and judge the reality in front of us.

How, then, can we move through our day-to-day lives without relying exclusively on conceptual interpretation? How can we find security and solidity and not feel vulnerable without it? Like an athlete who relies on their learned movements and an artist who is immersed in their creativity, we can embrace the transparent and spontaneous version of ourselves.

We use the intelligence that is inherent in consciousness to make calculations, for analysis, or to solve mathematical problems—as well as to decipher maps and to appreciate works of art, architecture, etc. However, we also use it to promptly create a series of movements and postures in our body when we practice a sport, carry out an artistic activity, or manufacture a gadget, for example.

More than once, it must have occurred to us that there is an intelligence in our mind, and this is not analysis, nor reason, but the part that knows what it has to do in the moment.

For example, on more than one occasion, we have had fun either playing with a ball or a racket, or riding a bicycle, etc. When doing these activities for the first time, we may have listened to someone's instructions or advice. And, at the time, we used our intelligence to analyze and understand what it was all about—or even to find our own techniques!

But, once we learned those techniques and felt comfortable with our mastery of the game or activity, there came a time when the analysis or judgment in the moment of the action, instead of bringing some benefit to the skill or ability, did the opposite: it limited or hindered us.

As we practice without the need for any analysis, our mind records in its consciousness the sequences of movements, positions, and displacements in the muscles and limbs of the body, among many other notions it perceives.

When, for example, we hold a basketball now, there is a perceptual register of when we held it on past occasions.

There is a record, in conscious memory, of how we feel when it is set in motion, of how we feel when we throw it away and when it returns to our hand, of the small impact and vibrations we perceive, and of many more aspects. Our mind perceives this information and much more—without resorting to analysis, judgment, or speculation.

The mind adapts and learns all these movements and, in turn, stores its experience in its conscious memory. Thus, when we perform the same activity again, our mind already has an experience of how the movements, balance, trajectories, etc, are perceived in the body.

The mind is versatile. In the middle of an activity, it pays attention to what it is executing in the moment and, at the same time, it uses the perception of body movement that is stored in its conscious memory from past experience.

There is a perceptual sequence recorded at the level of consciousness of the movements and this is what the mind transits through in the moment of action. While the physical body performs its movements, the mind is traveling within its perceptual experience.

However, the mind does not need to analyze in order to draw on these sequences of perceptual forms that have been recorded in its consciousness.

It does not access this perceptual memory through analysis. Rather, the record of the perceptual experience is already recorded in the conscious memory and remains at the mind's disposal whenever it is needed.

The mind follows a series of forms of its experience in the perception of movement in the muscles and limbs of the body, which comes through practice and accumulated experience.

It is like when a gymnast performs a floor routine. There is no room for analysis during the intensity, rhythm, and speed with which the body performs the sequence of exercises.

Once the routine begins, the gymnast can no longer be distracted by conscious thoughts about what they are doing. Rather, their attention is focused on the synchronization between their mind and the sequences of movements they must follow in the moment of the action.

Their mind follows the sequence that is recorded in their conscious memory, at the level of perception of the movement of the body, of each muscle involved in the execution of the exercises. That is, factors such as speed, balance, strength, etc, are recorded as perception in the conscious memory.

This perception possesses its own intelligence. The routine that is recorded in the consciousness at this level of perception is not that of reasoning, judgments, concepts, or thoughts.

Once the gymnast has begun their routine, each part of their body cooperates in synchronization with their mind. At every instant, the mind is focused on the sequence of movements they are executing with their body, which in turn draws on their experience in their conscious memory.

They cannot afford to make an elaborate judgment, even if they realize that things are not going according to plan. From their experience, they know that any judgment, self-reproach, or dissatisfaction that might arise from not performing as expected would only lead them to lose focus even more, which would surely mean more mistakes.

Practically, the mind no longer intervenes to create judgments, points of view, expectations, or speculations. Much of the mental activity that the concept of personhood brings has ceased. In its place, there is a mind that remains silent, attentive, and alert, flowing into what it does best in that moment. In mindfulness, the mind surrenders to follow in the perceptual sequence and synchronizes with the body, which then executes exactly what is required in each moment of the action.

It is the same mind that might be analyzing or making judgments under other circumstances, but now, during execution, it is employing the dynamism and harmony of the perceptual sequence in consciousness. Thus, while attention is prolonged in silence, the mind is functioning in a conscious medium and taking form in the grace and beauty that is generated by the efficiency with which the sequences of movements are being carried out.

It is thanks to the prolonging of attention that your mind synchronizes with your body to perform just what is required at each precise moment.

If the minds of athletes, musicians, artists, etc, enter into the immersion of prolonged attention, it is because they are disposing of the presence in their minds.

Now, the fact that the mind accesses states in which judgments and analysis cease to give way to full attention, harmony, and delight in efficiency is not exclusive to the performer who must memorize and follow to the letter the totality of movements that comprise their routine, as would be the case of a gymnast. It also happens in sports where the performer leaves room for improvisation where required.

Improvising in a sport means reading the situation so that a person can act according to what is required in the moment. However, even if there is no pre-established plan, the performer interprets the situation by digging into the experience accumulated in their conscious memory to decide what to do.

For example, a mountain biker descending a trail is looking ahead to recognize what the terrain demands. Thus, they can act with their technical resources and make use of the ability and dexterity that comes from their experience. This experience, held in their conscious memory, is the equivalent of a body language.

Winding through the trails at full speed, they make use of the expertise and skill they have acquired over their years of experience. As they descend the trail at full speed, they become aware of the terrain at a distance that allows them to anticipate and respond with the skill or technical resources the conditions demand. The circumstances require that the rider's mind maintain focused attention on the action in the moment.

Their mind searches, in its perceptual register, for sequences of movements, positions, rhythms, etc, that make up the dexterity and skill with which they dominate on their bicycle.

The cyclist executes what is required at that moment, without being distracted by judgment. In this way, even in the dizzying rhythm and rigor of physical demand in which the action takes place, their mind can access moments in states of full attention. The cyclist's mind enters an aura of stillness, silence, and harmony—as does the mind of so many people who have reached a high degree of mastery and who, in the midst of their performance, have their minds immersed in attention, enjoyment, harmony, and the beauty of what they are performing.

The jazz guitarist who, in the middle of improvisation, has their mind concentrated, absorbed in the instant of the action of their hands, performs almost automatically, recognizing the musical language that is stored in their conscious memory.

Their mind has forgotten their person. There is enthusiasm and confidence in a musical language. Concentrated attention arises in the perception of the precise movement of hands and fingers—fingers moving with agility and accuracy on the guitar, executing sequences of musical phrases.

It is a combination of executions at a high degree of complexity. Flashes of light, exhilaration, and enthusiasm between musical phrases ring in their minds. They experience an exchange of ideas, more light, empathy, generosity, absorption in the present moment and their fingers moving gracefully on the instrument.

A mind distracted by analysis, judgment, or speculative activity would not be able to execute with such precision and efficiency.

It is not the conditioned value of the mind that analyzes or speculates. The mind itself has taken a form where, within itself, there is harmony, beauty, grace, certainty, and delight in the music it is playing.

If athletes, musicians, artists, etc, delight us with a performance at a high level of complexity, it is thanks to the attention that is prolonged in a perfect mind-body synchronization.

And what is more interesting is that, when you enter this state of mindfulness, your mind automatically stops being distracted by concepts of yourself.

Flowing Close to the Being in Mindfulness

In our transparent self-identity, in which the ego loses strength and the essence shines through, we discover a source of wisdom, intuition, and vision that goes beyond words and analysis. A mind that enters this state, on the one hand, of prolonged attention, and on the other, of harmony and grace, is necessarily entering into consonance with the consciousness of its being.

If we adopt almost fully any one of these aspects of being, which are all part of the same existence, the others arise. The mind has several ways to come into consonance with the reality of harmony, grace, and the prolonged attention of its being.

Just like the athlete who trusts the movements that are recorded in their conscious memory or the musician who merges with the music emanating from their being, we too can trust our transparent and spontaneous instincts. In our transparent self-identity, we align with the flow of life, allowing the intelligence that inhabits us to guide our steps in harmony with the dance of being.

In that state, each moment becomes a performance: a work of art in which mind and body are one. The mind is not only a narrator but also a performer—an intimate collaborator with our inner presence and being.

Without having yet undergone the spiritual experience that is the awakening of the Divine spark within us, we can still approach that part of our mind where the presence and inner being coexist. We can adopt the version of our transparent identity, in which the concept of personhood is almost forgotten, and which remains innocent and spontaneous.

Where would this transparent identity of our person sustain their intelligence, their morality, their humanity?

The inner being is the source of intelligence that goes beyond mere analysis and reason. It is the abode of morality that emanates from a deeper understanding of the interconnectedness of all things. It is the essence of our humanity, which manifests itself in empathy, generosity, and love.

By embracing transparent self-identity, we allow ourselves to be more than the limitations of ego and conceptual labels. You become a being that is harmonized with the interplay of the aspects of the presence and inner being that reach behind your mind.

Contemplation - The Mental Witness

The position of the witness is the antechamber to the perception surrendered in the same consciousness of the presence; it is the passage that leads us to the perception of the Presence in its pure state.

In contemplation, the emergence of the full attention of the Presence—without executing a series of complex techniques—happens precisely because we are observing, from the position of the witness, the instant in which the mind pretends to identify itself with its subjective content, such as points of view or thoughts. That is where the attention of the witness, which originates in the Presence, resumes its existence.

We can expect there to be a significant approach to alert attention in the stillness and silence that leads to the perception of the presence when we manage to sustain the imperturbability, equanimity, and indifference of our witness.

The position of the witness is the path the mind naturally traverses to allow the reality of the presence to emerge, existing in the unfolding of the pure concentration of consciousness in a perfect present.

As the detachment is prolonged from the position of the witness, the moment arrives when the mind ceases to travel through the experience that was recorded in its conscious memory, and thus the perception of the presence arises, which is not misaligned with its existence in a perfect present.

Contemplation During Physical Exercise

Dynamic contemplation is the practice through which we adopt the position of the witness while engaging in a physical activity, such as walking, jogging, or running. We intentionally seek the conditions in which our mind will exercise the position of the witness in its alert and silent attention, while also sustaining a positive state of mind, even with the rigor and fatigue of the activity's physical demands.

We are going to seek to have our intense contemplation sessions in an outdoor space, where the witness part of the mind is exercised by dealing with a variety of stimuli, sensations and moods.

For example, if we jog, it is normal that halfway through the run, the physical strain may result in feelings of fatigue, discomfort, a decrease in our motivation, or even uncertainty, just to mention a few. In the midst of physical exercise, the witness part of our mind faces constant stimulation, not only due to the sensations of fatigue, discomfort and physical strain, but also due to moods and thoughts that may arise.

What we achieve, while we prolong the position of the witness that remains imperturbable and immovable in the midst of physical activity, is that the sensations of fatigue, strain and discomfort serve to accustom the mind to remain in the center, in its balance, in its equanimity, without giving up its good mood.

It is not expected that the arising sensations and moods will disappear. Even if we continue to feel tired, or experience sensations of muscle pain, or the desire to stop due to fatigue, without giving in to them, we maintain the witness part of our mind that is effectively detaching itself from the emotional dimension. It is difficult to notice the equanimity and silence of the witness consciousness while detaching itself from the constant stimulation that arises during physical activity. But we can be sure that, by remaining in the consciousness of the witness, we are strengthening imperturbability, detachment, equanimity, in addition to maintaining a positive emotional disposition, which are fundamental while entering into a state of deep meditation.

Cultivating equanimity and detachment in the face of a succession of feelings, moods and emotions, maintaining silent attention, in its center, in its balance, means an achievement for the witness part of our mind that will enter with ease into deep states of consciousness during meditation.

What happens, for example, if during our deep meditation session, we have already reached the imperturbable and immovable witness consciousness that remains in alert and silent attention, and suddenly we feel doubts or begin to lose interest—or we feel tired, bored, or uncomfortable because we have been sitting for so long?

Those impulses—those notions, sensations, and desires—could even present a greater distraction to the position of our witness on its journey, to acquire the perception of our presence, free from impulse and meaning, than thoughts or views arising in our mind.

The key is to bring to the meditation sessions a witness who can sustain, for a prolonged period, their alert attention, without being susceptible to falling into uneasiness, lack of interest or being distracted due to the discomfort that might arise from having been in the same physical position for a long time.

This part of our mind that adopts the position of the witness is the resource we possess to progress in this stage of purification of the mind, which is so important to initiate us in spiritual practice. With a dexterous, adept, and agile witness, we enter into the dynamism of the reality of the presence, which allows us to take that all-important step to transcend the notion of our "self."

CHAPTER 3

Consonance with Nature - Rebuilding our Link with the Presence

The mind that spends its time qualifying, making judgments, reasoning, building expectations, speculating, and involving its soul disposition in every aspect of life always possesses a wise presence—one that knows the route upon which it returns to the essence of its existence in consciousness.

Between the constant internal dialogue and the inertia of thought, we often forget our mind's innate ability to simply "be" - without judgment or interruption. Being in the here and now is an ability that is inherent in the mind's essential component of the presence.

Amidst the serenity of nature, our authentic "self" commits without the interference of judgments or expectations, resonating more with the here and now of the present moment. This alignment with an existence that is more in tune with presence allows us to perceive a reality beyond words and concepts, inviting us to embrace the beauty of experience without conceptual filters.

Have you ever wondered if we really must make every instant an occasion in which our mind interprets and applies meaning to everything it experiences, in a way that interrupts the free flow of consciousness?

Can we allow our mind to be aligned with tranquility, stillness, silence, equanimity, detachment—or an unconditional surrender to the subtle reality of its essence in consciousness?

When we sit in the grass, in a field somewhere, we feel in tune with the present moment. Our mind is silent, immersed in the here and now, without the distraction of judgments, concepts, or expectations. It is an experience of being authentic and innocent, of resonating with serenity and peace in the present moment, temporarily forgetting work troubles and social roles.

In those moments of silence, we live our existence far from the hustle and bustle of everyday life and the artificiality of the masks and roles we assume in society.

That is the enjoyment of being, utilizing all our available attention, interested in what we are witnessing.

In those moments, as we enjoy lying back, watching the sky and the clouds, is there a little inner voice that is still evaluating what is worthwhile, what is significant, and what is worth appreciating?

We may not recall this voice narrating the experience, or creating a representation of a moment that is originally spent in peace, in the calm and harmony that is inherent in our minds.

What we are witnessing does not require conceptual intermediaries, words, or language to keep us separated from the original perception in our minds.

Reality unfolds before us in silence, and our attention is immersed in the here and now, without the need to codify it or interpret it through concepts or words.

In this instant, we experience reality in the present moment. We are not encoding it or peeking at it through the keyhole of concepts, language, or words.

In this reality, we find intrinsic value, even in the apparent chaos and constant transformation. At that moment, we are not seeking to grasp reality with our comprehension in order to admire it. The reality that is in silence, free of meaning, is intrinsically worthwhile. It does not need us to qualify it, nor does it require conceptual interpretation.

In natural settings, our focus is recreated in a reality that is free of concepts. Our attention flows towards what resonates with the natural environment, where simplicity and authenticity are akin to our gaze.

There is something that captivates us in this simplicity, in which the reality that exists in nature is intrinsically worthy. The reality in which the elements are found in nature appeals to our mind. There is an implicit value in chaos, improvisation, and that which is constantly changing. There is an attraction to the likeness with which the elements exist in nature and the original, singular, emancipated part: the inspiration and intuition in our mind. By looking into nature, we find a reality that is more in tune with the freedom of our mind, its authenticity.

The authentic and emancipated version of our mind agrees with this reality. It moves away from the world of concepts in which it is forged by the conventions, idiosyncrasies, and conceptual masks of the sociocultural concept of our person.

We have been exercising the emancipated and singular part of our mind, so it is attracted to what it finds akin to it in reality.

This emancipated space already exists in our minds. It is an authentic and singular part: a part of us that, in silence, experiences moments of immersed attention, free of concepts. It consciously experiences instants of intuition, hunches, and vision that circulate without the interference of concepts.

Each person, in their mind, due to their nature in consciousness, has their emancipated part. Each mind has a peculiar way of expressing its unique existence.

It doesn't matter what nationality, gender, race, community, or even family we belong to. By our very nature in consciousness, there is always going to be a part of our mind that does not belong to any category. It belongs to itself: to the essence in its consciousness, to its freedom, its independence, its uniqueness, its vision, and its ingenuity. That is the value our mind carries. Each mind lives its emancipated part. Each mind has a unique way of experiencing reality. The perspective with which we take in the world every day is uniquely ours.

This part of the mind does not enter into any classification, nor does it enter into any role or concept of religion, politics, society, science, art, or philosophy. It exists by itself, free of concepts and directly experiencing reality.

We can use our mind to exert its influence in every moment, and we can also let it just be and exist.

The mind is more attuned to the cycles, changes, and transformations found in nature. It seeks a direct experience with reality. Our mind possesses a perspective that no longer clings to concepts to understand reality.

As it becomes more and more prominent, this original, singular, and emancipated part of our mind opens up to a perspective that no longer requires the shelter of concepts in order to interact with reality.

Everything you see in nature has an intrinsic value. Mountains are no more important than rivers. The sun shines no more for the rocks than for the bushes. We are all sharing the same space, existing in the same present, together with everything that encompasses our gaze.

The air we breathe is the same air that caresses the mountain peaks. Trees and plants come from the same earth we walk on and upon which other animals have walked. Mountains are neither feminine nor masculine.

Categorizations and concepts fade away.

Our mind feels comfortable appreciating that in which nothing is decided—a place where everything is in a delicate state of uncertainty that never ceases to find a new order.

The existence of the riverbed is humbly surrendered to the channel through which its torrent flows. It is an existence that is decided upon in each passing instant. So, too, the consciousness of the presence surrenders its attention to what our gaze perceives.

The mind, in its affinity with this uncertainty, unfolds into a range of possibilities. In this apparent equilibrium, a multitude of elements interact, reflecting the constant transformation of consciousness in our minds.

However, in those moments, the perception of the presence is not fully established. We overlook the idea that the stillness and silence of the mountains and, in general, of all of the natural scenery around us, are indications of the perception of our own presence.

The influence of the presence keeps the spaces of perception open, so the concepts do not distort the vividness of the natural scenery.

The subjective perspective of the mind is like a film that captures reality and transforms it into concepts, meanings, and familiar notions.

But the more we penetrate the stillness and silence of the presence, the more spaces open up where perception is no longer carried out from the format of emotional intelligence, and from specific points of view, concepts, or impressions.

There are intervals of silence and stillness that exist free of concepts. These spaces are small windows that lead to the consciousness of being.

That gaze, free of concepts, is the crack through which we add experience after experience to affirm the emancipated perspective that is aligned with our being. It is a space of consciousness that arises without meaning, and which opens up our minds.

Contemplation - Embracing Reality without Labels

Between nature in the environment that surrounds us and the observation of our mind, there is a bridge that invites us to cross it and takes us from the simple appreciation of reality to an introspective exploration of the perception and awareness of our being. This transition, between being present in the world and entering into the self that exists free of worldly and idiosyncratic conceptions, can be a transcendental experience. It is here that the act of contemplation takes on an essential prominence, as it allows us to immerse ourselves in the prolonging of inner silence. It is the state in which the position of the witness in peacefulness, equanimity, and calmness reigns and the conceptual interpretation of the mind is stilled.

In contemplation, we pause and allow the mind to be as close as possible to the attention that is prolonged in silence and free of meaning. We release the mind from having to elaborate on any point of view, and we accustom it to allow the present moment to pass as it exists in calmness, in sobriety, in silence. Free of thoughts, concepts, and impulses.

Our mind does not require us to transform the simplicity of the instant into the here and now, where it exists only by paying attention to something else. Therefore, we allow the mind to just "be" in the here and now. It has no task, just being and existing. In other words, during contemplation, we accept our mind in that stillness and silence, free of any interpretation. It does not have to inform us of anything. It does not have to function in order to tell us anything.

Whom must the mind serve, if we already adopt the position of the witness? The witness part of our mind that always pays an unperturbed and unmovable attention in peace and tranquility.

We expose our being to interact in the moment, in the here and now. That is our relationship with the moment. We shed the position taken by the mind that controls, that exerts its influence and rushes to form an interpretation. We observe the movement that the mind makes—that movement by which it tries to apply meaning and with which it seeks to recognize and interpret the thing we are witnessing.

We do not need to be the voice that quickly comes to create a story about or provide a description of that instant, since it only exists in attention and silence.

When our mind rushes to interpret what it experiences in the environment around us, we capture the instant with something we have created ourselves.

In this phase, we stop wanting the things we witness to conform to our conceptions of order. Order, from the perspective of being, is not conceptual; it is a reality of consciousness that exists in the harmony, peace, grace, and beauty that is prolonged by silent attention.

We leave at home the "expert" who classifies according to concepts. To interact with reality in the present, we bring not the scholar, but the wise presence.

Whatever conception we bring in the moment is lost from the existence to which our being is connected in silent attention.

Our inner witnessing mind, remains impartial, does not differentiate, nor does it bring to bear its tastes, interests, or preferences. The mental witness pays attention, in stillness and detached silence, quietness, and peacefulness. There is no desire, no stimulus, only acceptance. We observe every time our mind seeks to recognize according to a value, a purpose, a meaning, a reason, a utility, an object, or an end.

Again and again, the mind will try to capture the instant—which exists only in stillness and silence—with a concept, meaning, or thought.

We observe every impulse, notion, desire, and concept that passes through our mind to make it clear that we are the witness consciousness.

Thus, contemplation offers us the opportunity to highlight this movement in which part of the mind—not our inner witness—insists on capturing the present moment and transforming it into something of its own creation.

Our being is in its conscious medium while remaining attentive, as witness consciousness.

The present moment that passes in silent attention is the passage that leads us to the presence of our being.

We are, within our mind, observing what happens in the mind itself. We are not interested in interpreting with concepts what goes through our mind, but only in observing in order to detach ourselves and remain in the silent attention of the witness consciousness—the witness that remains unperturbed and only pays attention in silence.

We do not reject the thoughts, concepts, or notions that circulate, but rather we accept them without identifying with them. What is happening in that moment is that we are aware that we are the subtle consciousness of the witness that remains in alert attention.

We realize that the thoughts, concepts, or meanings that move through our mind are not necessarily our being. We are aware that we are the witness consciousness that remains attentive and exists independently of the subjective contents that transit through the mind.

The mental witness is the position that most closely resembles being in presence and that, at this stage, our mind can adopt. The position of the witness gradually restores our mind's awareness and brings it to concentrated attention, equanimity, and surrender of the presence.

Once we have realized that we are the witness who observes the thoughts that arise in our mind, we can open our eyes.

However, we can also close them whenever we want. But, by keeping our eyes open and prolonging our attention in silence while we become detached from what is going on in our mind, we have the opportunity to highlight the movement of the mind—that movement that seeks to capture the present moment with a meaning, point of view, or concept of its own understanding.

So, we open our eyes, and it is very likely that our mind rushes to bring us a point of view, with which it intends to replace the instant in which our being remains, paying attention in silence.

This movement of the mind—which seeks to anticipate with a meaning, impulse, or notion, and thus omit the instant in which it is, only attentively in stillness and silence—is the movement in which it generates a subjective perspective.

If we already realize that, apart from those points of view, we are the one who observes and pays attention in silence, without thoughts, when we open our eyes, we remain in the same position. We maintain the position of the witness, who remains attentive and alert, observing the thoughts, points of view, or concepts that pass through our minds.

What our witness consciousness observes, with its eyes closed, are the thoughts that pass through our mind. And, just as thoughts are only conceptual contents, so are the meanings, points of view, and notions that our mind could present when we open our eyes to the environment around us.

Whether our eyes are closed or open, the contents or conceptual forms that circulate use the same conscious medium: the attention of the witness consciousness in our mind.

If our thoughts have any relation to the reality of material objects in the environment around us, this relation is conceptual.

We are not waiting for the witness consciousness to become the same as the material reality of the environment. The fact that there is a conceptual relationship with the environment around us does not mean that our being can become the physical material plane of those objects. What our mind and its being do share with the environment around us and the material reality of the objects is their existence in the present instant.

In the same present instant in which our presence exists, the reality of the physical plane of matter is immersed, beginning with our body. All the elements of our body, including its organs, and the objects of the external environment are immersed in this same present instant in which our presence exists.

The trees, a dirt road, a lake, the places in our neighborhood, our house, or any other place … everything is immersed in this conscious and subtle reality that is the predominant component in our mind: the Presence.

So, when we open our eyes, our mental witness retains its position and observes, detached, every time our mind attempts to interrupt our attention in silence, in the here and now. We have already understood that we are the being that remains in stillness and silence—that which develops alert attention to the present moment and is free of meanings. Thanks to this, in the position of our witness we observe each time our mind tries to replace the passage, free of impulses and meanings, in which the presence exists in the here and now.

By prolonging the stillness and silence of witness consciousness, our attention becomes more and more alert and concentrated.

The position of the witness remains and observes every time the mind tries to bring forth a point of view, a concept, a notion, or an impulse, with which it seeks to capture and replace the instant that is passing in a state of attention and is becoming more and more alert.

Our witness is the part of the mind that exists in the present moment, developing as consciousness. The contents that transit as points of view, concepts, or impressions have always been inseparable from the instant in which our mind is only the alert attention in silence that originates in the Presence—the same Presence that exists and develops, uninterrupted, in the subtle reality of its consciousness.

Now, you have let go of the impulse with which your mind seeks to exert its influence on the peace and quiet of the here and now. You allow your being to exist according to its conscious nature.

In this moment, there is no notion of a "self" that brings its own elaboration into the silence of the consciousness that unfolds in our mind. We pay attention so that the moment—that instant in which our attentive mind passes in the here and now free of meanings—unfolds in a subtlety that does not include concepts or points of view.

We do not judge; we accept that subtle reality above any interpretation, point of view, concept, or impression that our mind brings.

We are the witness consciousness that remains equanimical. Our gaze does not look for differences. There is no difference between the stillness and silence of our witness and the instant that passes free of meaning in the external reality.

Our being is completely surrendered to the silent observer, to the witness consciousness.

Your being no longer serves the concept of your "self." In the prolonging of attention and silence, you allow it to unfold in the subtlety of its existence, in the consciousness that is its essence.

The impulses that usually tell your mind to look for some purpose, sense, reason, or end in that silence that passes without meaning have faded away.

You have ventured and allowed your being to be in the here and now, without differentiating from the present, which is free of meanings, along with the elements of the environment where you are.

A glimpse of your presence has already emerged, acquiring from its essence enough equanimity to remain unperturbed and immovable in its full attention.

You now possess a clear, pure, and alert mind that can follow the passing of the instant, in the here and now, in mindfulness.

The Mind and its Link with Existence

Having become imbued with the awareness of the presence, you have taken an important step towards the transcendence of your "self." You have learned to adopt the position of the witness, and from there, you have observed and detached yourself from the movements in which your subjective perspective is generated. You have penetrated into the subtlety of stillness and silence in which mindfulness unfolds your witness consciousness. To have been briefly in the full existence of the Presence, without the slightest trace of the notion of your person, is a powerful and transformative experience. With this clarity, we can begin to explore this new perspective. We enter a stage in which the process of transcendence that takes the being behind the mind gains momentum.

Without realizing it, behind the concept of "self," your being prepares itself to accommodate a new level of consciousness, closer to your presence, where authenticity and simplicity predominate, and where concepts are not necessary to live the truth that is the essence of your being. You are living the perspective of reality, which is in consonance with your original being, by putting it into practice. A dynamic part of your being is ready to vibrate according to the existential position you have discovered. Your wise presence has found its companion in that part of your mind that is agile, tenacious, and ready to assimilate the new existential position of your being.

In that sacred space of silence and clarity, we discover we have always been connected to the pure Presence: a state of being that transcends the ephemeral nature of thoughts and emotions. As we dive deeper, we begin to recognize that this pure state of the Presence has always been the essence of our existence.

We have not realized it before but, in part, our mind has always been in a pure state of the Presence. In fact, the main component of the thinking, feeling, and emotional mind is the Presence. The consciousness we experience when we pay attention or when our mind is immersed or absorbed is a partial state, inseparable from the pure state of the Presence.

In other words, it is the faculty with which we pay attention repeatedly throughout our day; it is an extension of the pure state of the Presence that exists continuously, without interruption, in a perfect present.

No matter whether our mind fluctuates between paying attention to the present moment, or being distracted by thoughts, feelings, emotions, impulses, or desires, there is always a degree of awareness. There is always a being that is, more or less, close to the pure state of the Presence.

Thus, in contemplation, we prolong our attention in silence and, with this, we allow the presence to emerge. In this way, we bring our mind closer and closer to the pure state of its presence. As the presence develops, our mind experiences the varying degrees of its attention. Our being goes through different levels of attention of the presence (immersion, absorption, mindfulness...)

until it becomes the same as the concentration of the Presence. The pure state of the Presence, by its nature, is not intermittent. It cannot be and also cease to be. The Presence can only manifest itself in extensions or partial states that are inseparable from its own pure Being. And, even in partial states where it differs from its pure existence, the Presence never ceases to exist. Since it enjoys an uninterrupted existence, there is no place or moment in which it is not developing in the concentration of its Consciousness.

Consciousness cannot arise from non-existence. We know we have consciousness, as we can verify that, in our mind, as well as in the mind of any other person, or even in animals, there is the capacity to pay attention, thanks to the Consciousness of the Presence. If this consciousness is one of the components from which our mind is made, this means that it also exists in its pure state.

By its nature, if the activity of a mind that creates conscious reality exists, this means it is an extension of the pure state in which universal Presence exists uninterrupted.

If, in our mind, we can partially experience what we feel as the present moment or as being present, it is because this notion comes from the existence of the Presence in its pure state.

It happens that, many times, we do not even realize our mind is coming into consonance with the reality of its components of consciousness.

It should not surprise us that, even when we are briefly immersed in enjoyment, feeling carefree, calm, and optimistic, or that nothing is missing, our mind is resonating in a state of consciousness that is closer to the being.

Mindful immersion, absorption, and attention are different degrees of the aspect of the Presence which, in its pure state, is concentration of consciousness, or Samadhi.

It is as simple as that occasion when you do not realize that you are, even briefly, immersed in your calm, your balance, or your optimism—that moment when you enter into consonance with the passage that leads you to adopt the perspective of the presence in your own mind.

We are, if only for a moment, immersed—whether in our calm, in our optimism, in our enthusiasm, in delight, or simply intrigued.

Our mind carries, inherent in its nature, in the consciousness from which it is made, this ability for immersion in attention, in optimism, in joy, etc. It does not need external factors. The being does not have to recognize what it believes to be the condition it deserves to exist in, according to its nature in consciousness.

In contemplation, we do not let the vagaries of circumstances or external factors dictate that our mind comes into alignment with the reality of the awareness of its being.

We practice, over and over again, our mind detaching itself from the functioning in which the concept of our "self" and its interpretive perspective are created.

We do not need any special ability, exceptional talent, or particular skill to do this. Our own presence knows how to transit and emerge into its conscious realm naturally. We all carry inside us a wise teacher, who stands alone as a witness and observes what passes in our minds. We detach ourselves from the subjective entity that yearns to exert its influence over every moment, allowing the witness part of our mind to bring us closer to the perception of true Presence.

There is no *who*, there is no notion of a person who is detaching from the impulses, the concepts, or the points of view that pass through our mind.

The wise Presence, this inner master, who emerges in equanimity, full attention, imperturbability, and detachment, has always been the main component of consciousness in our mind.

Through the simple fact that we perceive the peacefulness, calmness, stillness, and silence of our mind, which permeates the stage where we have directed our gaze, we are allowing our mind to be purified.

We purify our mind by becoming used to entering into consonance with this emancipated, self-sufficient part of it, which is not sustained by meanings or concepts.

It is purified because, by allowing it to resonate with the state in which it exists, its component of consciousness acquires and becomes imbued with the reality of its presence.

Our mind requires spaces where there is no need to enter into the interpretative activity with which it gives a meaning it brings from its accumulated understanding of conscious memory to each moment. The part of your mind that agrees and is more in tune with the emancipated, self-sufficient existence of the consciousness of your being does not need to resort to the intermediation of concepts to interact with reality in the here and now.

There is this part in our mind that is more in tune with our presence and accepts, without its interference, the way elements coexist in nature and reality in the here and now, completely free of meanings, concepts, or notions.

This version of yourself, in its authenticity, spontaneity, and innocence, does not categorize, does not make judgments, nor does it rush to exert its influence while witnessing the environment. The being is exposed, open, accepting the passing of the instant in the here and now, without interrupting its state of peacefulness, restlessness, stillness, and silence.

This is a relationship with existence in the instant, in the here and now, where the distinction of a "self" that exerts its influence by bringing some concept or point of view, making use of accumulated understanding, is not created.

CHAPTER 4

Empowering Your Inner Being - Strengthening the Being in Everyday Life.

In this chapter, we explore the reality of the authentic being that remains hidden behind our perceptions of the "self". Furthermore, we will understand that to reveal its reality in the subtle body that we carry within, internal reflection is not enough; It is essential to express our "self" in acts of love and service. This genuine being is nourished by our everyday experiences and seeks to transcend the concept we have of our identity, which strengthens our inner qualities, such as generosity, honesty, and goodwill.

So the question arises: How can we reflect our being in every act, every word, and every glance? The answer lies in shedding our old identity and embracing an authentically spontaneous and transparent version of ourselves that goes beyond individuality. In our daily lives, we exercise the noble identity.

In life itself, and in our service, work, activities, etc, we have the spiritual energy of our inner being at the level of consciousness. By having our human qualities at our disposal, the being, at the level of consciousness, is weaving the pathways that will later serve it in deep meditation. Thus, our being becomes the fruitful medium of consciousness for the union of presence and the Divine spark that we carry in our subtle body.

The serenity, balance, and equanimity which has permeated our mind at the level of consciousness weave a fabric of fruitful pathways at this consciousness level. These are the vibrant and glistening pathways that have been opened by having continuously made use of the generosity, honesty, openness, and goodwill at their source in the Divine spark that we carry within our inner being.

Thus, at the level of consciousness, pathways are created so that, in deep meditation, the presence merges with the being that is all provider of love—with the Divine spark that dwells in the body of consciousness that we carry within—aspiring for the Will of the most benevolent, generous, truthful, and reliable Being. The Mother of Consciousness. The Divine Mother.

Life experience causes us to draw upon and utilize that which originates in the very consciousness of the inner being, at the core of which dwells the spark of the Divine. This is the mission of the human mind that inhabits a physical body. The human mind comes to this world to open the pathways in the consciousness that is its essence, in which the presence and the Divine spark merge.

Without realizing it, we possess human qualities at the consciousness level of being that are always within our mind. The manifestation of these qualities depends on the work we do to cultivate them.

As we understand the importance of cultivating these virtues, contemplation emerges as an essential tool. By purifying the mind and consolidating these qualities, we create a conscious environment that is conducive to the emergence of the most authentic aspiration and surrender to the love of the Divine Being in deep meditation.

Consider that, at the level of consciousness, the being bridges the gap between the dual aspect of the presence and the fertile conscious medium of the inner being, which carries the Divine spark at its core. There, the present instant of the presence and the fruits of the human qualities that originate in the inner being intertwine at the level of consciousness.

Through contemplation, we purify the mind. And, in doing so, the pathways that have been forged by having the fraternity, determination, self-sufficiency, and willpower in our daily lives become within reach of the presence.

The presence with which our mind is imbued is the best ally of our human qualities. After contemplative practice, we return to the activity of our daily life knowing that, at the level of consciousness, the presence with which our mind is imbued is weaving a link with the pathways of our goodwill. The presence penetrates the conscious medium that we forge by having the goodwill and nobility that originate from the inner being.

Our goodwill and nobility are no longer deferred through valuation, judgments, or expectations. Now, thanks to the influence of the presence, these qualities manifest in our daily life, in the here and now.

Everything goes together in the authentic, spontaneous, and innocent version of our person—the longing and aspiration for fraternity among people, for the common good, for solidarity, and for the frankness that we maintain in our relationships with other people, the goodwill in our dealings, and the nobility of our intentions and motivations.

Presence becomes the best container and ally of our talents, desires, aspirations, and the roles we play in our daily lives.

By purifying the mind in contemplative practice, the path of the being that seeks to transcend the current notion of "self" gains momentum in consciousness.

Transformation happens naturally. Within our mind, necessary changes take place that are also reflected in the person who serves in the community. The notion of our "self" has always made use of the component of the consciousness of the being to feel empathy and to feel connected to the lives of people who are close to us. However, when spiritual awakening comes, we understand that, much like the awakened being, human qualities have no other owner than the Divine Being from which the reality of consciousness, the Divine Mother, originates. The being that is pure love goes into the core of our inner being, into the subtlety of the Divine spark with which the presence unites when it arises from deep meditation.

The purification that we carry out during contemplation prepares us, so our mind can allow the notion of our "self" to fade away and the presence to emerge. This condition is indispensable for spiritual awakening to occur in deep meditation.

In other words, both conditions are indispensable: on the one hand, our mind is shaped by life experience and, on the other hand, by the ability to allow the presence to emanate and blur the notion of our "self."

We contemplate and, by allowing even a glimpse of the presence to emerge, we know that it receives our nobility and our human qualities in its present. Thus, even though the presence and the spark of the Divine, that exists in the subtlety of the inner being have not merged, by allowing even a small part of pure consciousness to emerge in our mind, they are aligned in the position where the dual aspect of the presence and the inner being converge.

The synergy of the components of the presence and inner being, which at its core carries the Divine spark, gains momentum. The influence of the being is strengthened. No matter where we are or where we go, the components of the consciousness of the presence and the inner being that carries the spark of the Divine are always within us.

By carrying out the contemplation sessions with our eyes open, we get used to extending the perspective of the presence in life in the here and now, in our occupations, work, labor, and service. We test, again and again, the authentic, spontaneous version that serves its community in goodwill. The transformation that takes place through intense contemplation sessions, at the consciousness level allows the being to gain momentum in our day-to-day situations.

As the being gains prominence in our mind, it enlightens us through its inquiries, revelations, intuition, and vision. This means that we also carry within the being a psychologist that is custom-made to what our mind requires in order to progress in our spiritual development. The discoveries of our being have the power to remove impediments and imperfections at the level of consciousness. It silently reveals and enlightens us, facilitating our progress towards deciphering our notion of "self" at the consciousness level.

We carry in our own mind the wise presence that, by its nature, knows how to remain in full attention in the here and now—and also the inspiration, intuition, vision, and love of the inner being. By allowing our mind to be impregnated with the wise presence, through the intensive practice of contemplation, we also allow more frequent moments of inquiry, enlightenment, inspiration, intuition, and vision.

This is why there is no better teacher than our own presence and the intuition, hunches, vision, and enlightenment that come from the inner being. In the dual aspect of our being, we possess wisdom in its dynamism, that removes what prevents the pure state of its essence from emerging in this unique pattern of consciousness that is the notion of our "self."

The reality of being dismantles the pattern of consciousness of the emotional intelligence, vital, and subconscious realms in which the notion of the "self" is generated.

Everything is devoid of concepts. Everything unfolds in the wise practical dynamism of the mind, which acquires from the presence the impetus it needs to move toward the transcendence of the notion of "self."

By allowing even a hint of the perspective of the presence to emerge, the influence of the being is prominent in our life, accelerating the process by which our mind acquires the conditions for deep meditation and the spiritual awakening to come.

It is our wise presence that will carry out the transformation and the arrangements that are required to accelerate the process in which we acquire the necessary conditions so that, when the time comes to initiate the sessions of deep meditation, our mind knows the way to blur the notion of our "self."

Taking prominence in our being, the reality of our presence—the experience of our daily life—will add, through our renewed perspective, to intensify elucidation by removing false conceptions, imperfections, and impediments that could obstruct the progress that our being takes to transcend the notion of our "self" at the level of our consciousness.

The true being remains imperceptible, but at the same time, knows how to add to its cause by taking advantage of what is happening in our day-to-day life.

The sage within us leads us—if we allow it to exert its influence—in the direction of fulfilling its objective of transcending the mental notion of "self".

The being, which resembles a catalytic element at the consciousness level, takes from the experience, situations, and circumstances of our day-to-day life to contribute to the process of deciphering the notion of our "self."

To achieve this, it needs our service. It places us in service—and, when in service to the community at the level of consciousness, we help the being to dismantle the notion of a person that has been created and recreated in the idiosyncratic lifestyles of the collective.

If the wisdom of the being deems it necessary, it will strip us and lay us bare. We will find ourselves in a series of situations that challenge the "self," in which it will have no choice but to be humble, sensible, and constantly have its willpower at its disposal. For example, it will distance us from the illusion of the consumerist life.

We will have to muster all the will, skill, ability, kindness, and generosity at our disposal and put them in service of the transformation that is taking place in the self.

Our goodwill and our human qualities no longer belong to the concept of a person. There is a detachment, a service in letting go.

We realize that our person is the more spontaneous and humbler version of us—that identity which was sacrificing itself in service to its community. One which has already traveled a good stretch of the path in austerity and in sacrifice, constantly drawing on the willpower that originates in our spirit.

The concept of our "self" that had to be released is no longer anchored to the ideas, expectations, values, and temperament of the collective. At the consciousness level, our presence has been interacting with an emancipated, authentic, and self-sufficient "self" that no longer needs to sustain its value, confidence, and sense of belonging in the idiosyncrasies of the collective.

With this, the process has been streamlined that allows the presence to decipher the concept of a "self" constructed from a variety of roles, characters, forms, styles, and mannerisms that circulate in the collective.

The Pathways towards Pure Aspiration and Surrender

Our purification and life experience, where we have made use of our willpower, self-sufficiency, talent, courage, and humanity, have opened the channels that will serve to generate the purest aspiration and surrender to the Divine Will.

Our mind is almost ready to serve as a means for what is engraved in the nature of the Presence and the spark of the Divine to take place in deep meditation. Your goodwill, which you have put to service in the community, has borne fruit. It was already the means of experiencing the fertile consciousness that gave you access to the Presence in deep meditation to discover the spark of the Divine in your subtle body.

Now, the conditions are being prepared at the level of consciousness, where the Presence merges with the Divine spark, in the spiritual awakening that occurs in deep meditation.

The components of the presence and the inner being of your mind have always been an extension of the merged state in which the awakened being exists. Spiritual awakening had not yet occurred. However, at the level of consciousness, the conditions were already in place so that, in deep meditation, the witness part of our mind was able to blur the notion of our "self", allowing the presence and the Divine spark in our inner being, to enter into the interaction dictated by their conscious nature.

At the level of consciousness, both the presence and the consciousness of the inner being arrange to create the conditions in which, without the slightest intervention of our "self," they can unite in spiritual awakening.

The pathways are open at the level of consciousness. They are pathways imbued with the consciousness of the inner being because we have been constantly drawing upon the energy of our being. It is the energy of the spark of the being, which harmonizes everything, links everything, and provides us with the purest love. It is a wise energy that originates in the Divine spark and manifests itself in our willpower, generosity, detachment, freedom, self-sufficiency, and determination.

The dual aspect of the presence and inner being intensifies their synergy. The equanimity, humility, stillness, and silence of the presence shorten the distance to the love that originates in the Divine spark, thus tightening their bond.

The influence of being gains strength and thus prevents the penetration into our mind of what is out of tune with the conscious field.

It only remains for us to bring it into the sanctuary of deep meditation. Thus, the force of the synergy of the presence and the inner being that is carried at the consciousness level in our mind will be able to enter into the interaction that is engraved in its nature.

The experience of unveiling the Divine spark of our inner being during deep meditation does not correspond to the perspective in the emotional intelligence realm in which we comprehend ourselves and the environment around us.

In the contemplative practice, we rehearse adopting in a stable and prolonged way the position of our witness, with which we prepare our mind to enter into perception in the subtle plane of the consciousness of our presence.

It is from the perception of the presence that our mind can enter into the subtle plane of consciousness, where the inner being that houses the spark of the Divine that exists within our physical body.

Existence in Pure Consciousness

After this process, through which we have navigated the depths of being and the presence in the everyday scenario of life, we find the threshold of a sacred sanctuary: deep meditation. This is a space where conditions align to allow the linking of the components of the being, which by their nature in consciousness, are destined to unite.

In deep meditation sessions—by adopting the position of the witness and focusing our alert attention towards the interior of our body, in the center of the chest at the level of our heart, and with a perfect surrender to the love of the Divine Being—we perceive the subtlety and unveil what is barely a spark, yet that which is the link we have with the Cosmic Divine Being.

The reality of consciousness, in which the components we carry of the presence and inner being merge, is in the unfolding of consciousness in a perfect present.

It is in the here and now of the Presence, in the concentration of its consciousness and when its pure state emerges, that the condition is provided for the interaction with the inner being to come about, without the least intervention of the notion of our person.

At this moment, we are governed by the designs of consciousness in its state which is already liberated from the emotional intelligence sphere in which our thoughts, emotions, impulses, or desires were happening.

Consciousness is stripped of the veil that had it conditioned and programmed to generate a subjective perspective of the present moment.

The entity, maintaining a distance from its own existence in pure consciousness, dissolves.

Presence, when it emerges in its pure state, can only unfold, and concentrate on the subtle plane of consciousness.

Since we begin to meditate, we adopt the position of the witness in detachment, in its imperturbability, and at the same time we focus its attention concentrated inside our body, at the level of the heart in the middle of the chest. In that position the divine spark is lodged in the subtlety of the inner body.

As it acquires the alert concentration that flows free of meaning, we surrender and aspire that it be only the Will of the Divine Being.

We expect nothing; we leave everything in the hands of the Divine Mother. The notion of our "self" is blurred, and we let go of any influence that our mind might pretend to exert. We leave it to the freedom of the consciousness components of presence and the inner being to enter into the interaction that is dictated by their nature in consciousness.

Presence and the Divine spark, by their nature in consciousness, are destined to merge.

The merged state is that of the awakened being. It is in this same merged state that the Cosmic Divine Beings exist, continuously unfolding in the higher planes of consciousness.

In deep meditation, the full attention of the Presence emerges, which occurs free of thoughts, impulses, and meanings. The witness consciousness remains undisturbed and self-contained, while observing the subjective contents that pass through the mind. Now, the inner witness mind engages in the purest surrender to the development that occurs in the concentration of consciousness.

At that moment, we no longer "are." The notion of our "self" has blurred. Our subjectivity has vanished; it is completely dissolved. In its place, there is only the presence that surrenders to the Will of the Divine Mother in our Divine spark.

One must have full trust in the Divine Being. At that moment, the being that is unfolding in the subtle reality of consciousness surrenders unconditionally to the will of the kindest, most benevolent, most loving being, who awakens the spark of the Divine within our physical body.

We surrender unconditionally to the Will of the Divine Mother, concentrated in the subtlety of the divine spark we perceive in our inner being. In the purest surrender and in the truest aspiration, the being is only the Will of the Divine Mother in the spark of the Divine of the subtle body, at the level of the heart, in the center of the chest.

The perception of the presence on the subtle plane of consciousness, where the Divine spark is unveiled, is a state of existence that has always been within reach of our minds, waiting to be discovered. It is where the synergy between the presence and the divine spark merge, giving birth to a new existence: the awakened being, taken from the grace of the Divine Mother, undertakes its evolutionary transformation in the physical body.

The Instrument of the Divine Mother

Now, with the awakened being attached to the subtle plane of consciousness, our being is ready to explore the realities that are accessed by the being that supports, sustains, and lovingly procures the reality of consciousness. The awakened being is linked with the existence of the Divine Being, in the planes in which the reality of consciousness originates. There, it surrenders itself fully to the Divine Will. The consciousness of the awakened being has arisen and that reality is now the one that leads us.

The spiritual awakening has taken place and the being that now exists within our physical body is a new one.

How could we have imagined that this body of ours, which has existed throughout all these years of life experience as productive people who are part of a family and a society, would now carry a being that experiences a new way of perceiving and existing in this world?

The change that has occurred was caused by the spiritual awakening and the subsequent experiences that have transformed this being. This being is the same mind that, before, never ceased to be engaged in the drama of a "self." At all times, within this mind, there were the components in the presence and consciousness of the inner being that, even without having been fused, belonged to the conscious reality in which the awakened being exists, accessing the levels of consciousness in which the Cosmic Divine Beings exist, uninterrupted.

Without realizing it throughout all these years, our minds were being carved in ways that, in deep meditation, would serve to enliven the most intense and authentic aspiration in the unconditional surrender to the love of the Divine Being.

Prior to spiritual awakening, life experience has been made constantly available to us, at the consciousness level in our mind; the kindness, generosity, openness, freedom, self-sufficiency, and willpower provided by the consciousness of the inner being within our body.

We have kept the conscious medium of our mind nourished by making use of the consciousness that originates from the inner being, which carries the spark of the Divine at its core.

There was goodwill in the roles and characters we played in our daily lives, and in the intentions, motivations, and longings.

Now, after the spiritual awakening, in subsequent meditation sessions, we can resume the position where our being is awakened. The awakened being becomes the instrument of the Divine Mother. Already merged in spiritual awakening, our being can enjoy the consciousness of the Divine Being that exists in all its splendor, glory, Divine grace, and ecstasy, in the higher levels of consciousness.

In meditation, we surrender to the awakened being so that the Will of the Divine Mother can take it and use it in her project of spiritual evolution.

Everything acquires its correct value. We are even grateful for the training we have received from the facet in which our mind created and recreated the notion of our "self," based on the idiosyncrasies of its community. We are very grateful for those ideas, customs, expectations, and values, and for the temperament and feeling of the community. This is because, whether they contributed as impediments or as opportunities, they had to do with generating the conditions for spiritual awakening to come later.

At the level of consciousness, that notion of our "self" that we produced as a function of the idiosyncrasies of our society was what our being dealt with again and again. That notion of our "self" was, at the same time, the impediment and the set of our talents, abilities, skills, longings, motivations, and intentions with which the consciousness of our being interacted.

Because it is precisely in the opposition, resistance, impediments, etc, that occur in our existence that the movement of being that seeks to decipher the concept of our "self" gains momentum.

If there is a constant with which the being that incarnates in a physical body and comes to this earth to undertake the adventure that is life, that constant is resistance.

How will the being seek to transform something if there is no resistance, if it does not find impediments in what our mind is composed of at the level of consciousness? From the notion of our person, the being knows how to take advantage of what it contributes to the process of transcendence that it is carrying out.

We must not lose sight of the fact that, without this original and unique person that is our "self" at the level of consciousness, the being would not be taking decisive steps to transcend it.

The concept of our "self," the person we are with all our talents, virtues, limitations, and defects, is already responding to the influence of the being.

We must also not forget that all this is happening while our "self" is leading a productive life in society, and existing according to its yearnings, aspirations, and motivations.

It is likely that what we experience in daily life also contributes to our willpower, determination, courage, talent, authenticity, humility, selflessness, and generosity.

CHAPTER 5

The Path Towards the Awakened Being

Pure consciousness, guided by the wisdom of the being, provides the opportunity for a fundamental change in our perception of the world and ourselves. We will now explain the essential conditions we must establish before we immerse ourselves in deep meditation.

A good practice to unseat the subjective functioning of our mind in our meditative sessions is to prepare the conditions in equanimity, in silence, in acceptance, in good sense, in that precious time, which is when we are engaged in our work.

We prepare the conditions during our day-to-day activities, and thus in meditation sessions, we facilitate the emergence of the perception of the presence, which overcomes the subjective functioning of our mind.

While we are busy with our activities, an effective way there is to detach from the thoughts that take us from our center of harmony is to observe them from the perspective of an active witness in compassion.

Compassion must first be practiced in our own thoughts, and at that very moment, the part of ourselves that is closest to the origin of love in our inner being is revealed.

We must have compassion—and, if possible, even sympathy—to be able to accept those thoughts and emotions and give them their fair value, while we observe them without identifying with them.

Having compassion and sympathy for our feelings, thoughts, and emotions does not mean we identify with them; we accept them, seeing them from a perspective of tolerance, understanding, and love.

If we have sympathy for them, we accept them, we understand them and we find their gentle side. We may even observe them with curiosity and humor, and this does not mean we identify with them. In the same detachment that occurs when we adopt the witness position, we bring our good mood to the process. It's like when we take with humor the thought or the idea that we came up with.

We return to our good mood, with which we enter into harmony with the influence of the inner being by observing our thoughts with compassion, sympathy, tolerance, and understanding, in love.

So, this daily exercise that we do, of observing our own thoughts, accepting them with compassion and sympathy, automatically puts our good mood in the forefront, making it easier to preserve the harmony, peace, and love that is inherent to the inner being. What is more, when there is peace, harmony, and love, our mind naturally resonates in the here and now, in the stillness and silence of the witness consciousness, which originates in the presence.

The Inner Witnessing Mind

In contemplative practice, we foster moments in which we set aside the interpretative mind. We allow the witness part of our mind to take prominence. By adopting the position of the witness, we nullify the activity of our mind that seeks, according to its expectations, to reestablish its value, esteem, certainty, and sense of belonging by involving its emotional mood.

The inner witnessing mind, in its equanimity, imperturbability, and immobility, accepts the instant that passes just as it is, annulling the impulses, desires, and demands of our persona. This is the entirety of the subjective activity of our mind.

Therefore, we have already dedicated a good amount of time, with regularity and perseverance, to contemplative practice, and we have accelerated the purification of our being. In fact, through contemplative practice, we have been purifying our being, experiencing glimpses of the aspects of equanimity, stillness, silence, mindfulness, acceptance, and surrender of the presence.

Likewise, in contemplation, we rehearse again and again our entrance into the state of mindfulness, in the detachment of the concepts and sense that generate the notion of our "self." We also acquire the ability to prolong attention that is free of meaning so that, in deep meditation, the awareness of the presence emerges.

On the other hand, thanks to purification, the conditions of surrender and aspiration are already sufficiently given so that, during deep meditation, the union of the presence and the spark of the Divine takes place.

In this way, we are ready to surrender our presence to the Will of the Divine during deep meditation. And, during deep meditation, our presence is surrendered in the most intense aspiration for the love of the being. That is, the presence has surrendered to that being which is pure goodness, truthfulness, love, certainty, and abundance, through the attraction of the Divine spark of our inner being at the level of the heart, in the center of the chest.

By concentrating its attention within, on the inner being, the already liberated presence has enough sensitivity to perceive the subtlety of the spark of the Divine, since it corresponds to its reality in consciousness.

When the presence surrenders to the purest aspiration, it is such an intense feeling that its union with the Divine Mother becomes irreversible. An intense aspiration arises for that moment to be nothing more than the Will of the Divine Mother, in the Divine spark, and attraction in love, truthfulness, certainty, and abundance.

That is why, in contemplation, we try to allow our mind to blur the notion of our "self." Thus, later, in deep meditation, our being can be the conscious means that remains surrendered, in the purest aspiration, to the Will of the Divine Being, so the link between the Presence and the spark of the Divine can take place.

When the spiritual being in us is awakened, we access the planes of consciousness where the Cosmic Divine Being exists.

This is because the configuration of consciousness of the reality of the Divine Being is the fusion of the Presence and Divine spark.

Purification establishes the necessary conditions for the union of the presence and the Divine spark to be realized during deep meditation. We are now ready to surrender our presence to the Will of the Divine.

The Awakening of the Inner Being

The union of the presence and the spark of the Divine manifests itself as a natural courtship, driven by a deep and irreversible attraction. This union is completely guided by the Divine Will. The presence surrenders deeply to the love of the being. We experience a complete surrender to the Will of the Divine, which manifests in one or the more of the following: love, certainty, peace, grace, joy, and ecstasy of the Divine Consciousness, a spark of which resides in the heart of our being. We are ready to deepen the connection with our inner being and experience the subtlety of the spark of the Divine.

In deep meditation, simultaneously, as the notion of our "self" dissipates, we enter into the most authentic surrender to the Will of the Divine. We allow the purest and most authentic surrender and aspiration to the Divine Will to arise.

As the witness part of our mind emerges in perfect silence, its concentrated attention is directed towards within the physical body, in our inner being, at the level of the heart, in the center of the chest where the spark of the Divine is located.

Everything happens in mindfulness: in perfect silence, free of thoughts, with the most authentic aspiration to be nothing

The Path Towards the Awakened Being

more than the Will of the Divine Mother. At that moment, we surrender unconditionally to the Will of the kindest and wisest, the most loving, generous, and truthful being. We leave everything in the hands of the Divine Mother, who knows how to give us the exact spiritual experience we need to progress in our level of consciousness.

If our mind intervenes with its imagination, it only hinders the process. We do not need to add anything; we accept the subtlety of consciousness as the only reality. We allow the Divine Will to be done. We simply initiate the process; we do not interfere in the interaction that is called for by its conscious nature, the presence and Divine spark in the subtle body.

The witness consciousness has emerged, absolutely surrendered, and available to interact in the subtle reality in which it unfolds in our inner being, the spark of the Divine. There is not the slightest interference of the notion of our "self." It has already yielded. For some time now, the subjectivity of our mind and the sense of our "self" have been blurred and have given way to the absorption of the concentration of the pure consciousness of our presence. Our mind has entered the state of Samadhi and has secured its good fortune by surrendering completely to the Divine Will that is at the level of our heart, in the center of our chest, in our inner being.

In Samadhi, there is no longer the notion of our "self." It is the trance of the presence that is absorbed and occurs in the concentration of its consciousness. There is no longer a reality that resembles the concept of our person. Our body is there, but our mind has already yielded completely to the concentration of consciousness that is about to unite with the divine spark.

The original surrendering of our presence arises. At this point, we cannot say that our person has surrendered, since the notion of our person is already behind us. Now, it is the surrender in which the presence exists by its conscious nature.

The subjectivity of our mind ceases, so that the concept of our "self" is blurred. In its place, there is a very attentive, alert, and conscious perception that is free of meaning. At that moment, that stillness and silence of the subtle plane of consciousness is our entire reality. We accept it completely, unconditionally surrendering, without waiting and without trying to understand it. It is a moment of absolute humility and unconditional surrender to the Divine Will.

It is the most authentic aspiration to the Will of the Divine Being because the subjective mind of our "self" does not participate in the least. It is the surrender and aspiration to the Divine Will that is inherent to our being.

The presence and the Divine spark are called to unite. They enter into their courtship. They carry out the interaction that is engraved in their consciousness. Their attraction is irreversible. It is only the Will of the Divine that intervenes.

There is a complete surrender to the Divine Will, and our being takes the level of consciousness in the intensification of feelings of one or the combination of love, certainty, peace, grace, joy, glory, and ecstasy of the Divine Consciousness at the height of our heart, in the middle of the chest, in our inner being.

The presence perceives in the subtlety of the consciousness of the inner subtle body, thus revealing the Divine spark. From the fusion emerges the awakened being that begins its evolution toward the higher planes of consciousness.

Emerging in the Divine Consciousness

As we go through this profound process of surrender and union, we emerge with a new being, where the perspective of the awakened being reigns supreme.

Transformation occurs when the presence and the Divine spark merge; this transformation leads to the awakened being, which begins its evolution into the planes of consciousness of the being in which it originates. In this experience, everything unfolds in the context of the Wisdom of the Mother of consciousness, who sustains and provides for us with love. Everything unfolds in the conscious medium of the Divine Mother, who waits patiently in the consciousness of each individual's being.

The awakened being is the same conscious medium of the mind. Although not fused by spiritual awakening, the consciousness components of our mind—in the presence and in the inner being—correspond to the reality of the awakened being and the Cosmic Divine.

That person who sought to reinvent themselves by changing their image, lifestyle, ideologies, philosophies, or membership in a social circle carries in their mind the components of the presence and the Divine spark. And, if these are united in the spiritual awakening, they become the most forceful, concrete, and renewing experience.

We no longer need to look to external conditions or factors, since the awakened being has at its disposal the totality of the reality of consciousness. At that moment, that being is what we are. This entity of awakened consciousness is the most transformative, abundant, and truthful subtlety of our existence.

Thus, once the inner being has been awakened by the union of the presence and the spark of the Divine, we can take up its purest reality in meditation. And it is enough for us to go a little deeper into our being to experience more intensely and concretely the reality of consciousness in which it exists.

What is happening now is that the components of consciousness in the presence and the core of our inner being, the spark of the Divine, have merged. The same components of consciousness that, without being united, served the realm of emotional intelligence to occupy it in its subjective perspective are now fused. Thanks to this, a complete, active being has emerged that remains and exists from its conscious perspective.

Before the spiritual awakening, how could we imagine that our mind could also be the consciousness that comes from the higher planes where the Divine Being dwells?

How could we believe that this perspective, with which we experience every moment of our day, would be an overflowing existence, in harmony, love, peace, balance, and always in a present that is free of concepts?

We had no idea that the same mind that always told us "You are this person" and "You had these tastes, preferences, interests, and convictions" would be able to attain an existence where the "self" is suspended and we are only a complete reality of consciousness, whole and full of truthfulness, certainty, abundance, and peace.

How could we imagine that our mind could detach itself from the functioning in which, at every moment, it seeks to reestablish its value, certainty, confidence, esteem, and sense of belonging?

The awakened being, as it emerges, inhabits what the mind of the notion of our "self" sought in what it understood as the value of our existence and our love. It unfolds according to its own design, following the wise intelligence in the reality of consciousness.

Is there a mind seeking to reestablish its value, esteem, and sense of belonging?

We have occupied the components of the presence and consciousness of the inner being, imbued with the Divine influence on this mind, to generate the concept of a person who based their value and esteem on achievement, recognition, status, prestige, and power. Now, by remaining in the presence, we enter into the existence of this being, according to its conscious nature, free from the sociocultural and worldly idiosyncrasies on which our person was based. It understands the reality of the ego's concepts and feelings. It understands subjective reality, but when the being emerges, it exists in consciousness, in harmony, peace, certainty, and abundance.

Is there a concept of a "self" that interprets according to what it understands about gender, nationality, race, and social status—and political, religious, or other types of affiliation?

Spiritual awakening initiates a new stage of transformation and discovery for our being.

The mind that believed that its reality was its gender, nationality, race, community, and belonging has been transformed by spiritual awakening into a servant of the plan of the Divine Being, in which consciousness originates. It supports, sustains, provides with its care, and makes possible that which concerns the reality of consciousness—the conscious substance of which the mind and the inner being are composed in the human body.

Before awakening, the "self" believed that its existence was limited to what affected the reality of the physical body and the mind that provided the notion of a person, a story, a drama, roles, and characters. Now, an awakened being follows its design in the evolution of consciousness.

Experiencing the levels of consciousness, it discovers what its being always was. It discovers its being in its origin, taking existence in each reality that it accesses of the Divine Being. The awakened being discovers and is coupled with the realities in which the Divine Mother exists—the reality in which it is composed and where the Divine Being unfolds in the higher planes of consciousness.

Does this fulfilled being need to calculate, qualify, or judge anything? A being in this physical body unfolds in the instant, here and now, immersed and flowing along with the presence in the environment.

In the awakened being, we enter into the reality where everything that sustains this creation is within that subtlety. We can see through the existence of this being and look around at the setting. But it is also enough just to be, without seeing, without hearing, without touching. Everything we need is there, within its consciousness.

But how can we not enjoy living with our eyes wide open, delighting in what it reveals to us when we exist from its perspective? A consciousness occurring clean of thoughts, delighting in being what it is.

It unfolds in the home, in the medium of consciousness of its existence. The body that carries it is irrelevant, grateful for allowing it to see and experience in full color the beauty of forms in nature.

Our gaze becomes the conscious medium that does not interrupt the present instant with meaning, but allows grace and beauty to flow. It does not bring an interpretation of its own elaboration of beauty. It lets beauty, grace, and harmony unfold in consciousness, without interruption.

The perception of the being occurs in the grace of the cosmic Being, which is pure harmony and grace. The being is immersed in the conscious medium of which it is made. It has detached itself from the interpretation of the subjective mind. Its existence unfolds, free of meanings, like a blank canvas full of existence.

This is its present. The tireless creator of subjective scenarios ceases. It is resting.

This new way of experiencing reality is no longer the subjective perspective in which our mind and what it saw were in its own image and likeness.

There are no meanings of an experience of the "self" that pretends to anticipate and make that instant that flows in the consciousness of the Divine Mother something of its own creation.

The level of consciousness in which our being flows does not carry concepts to interpret and transform this cosmic perspective into a point of view that is informed by the notion of a "self."

Our being flows in its own elixir. Within that subtlety lies the greatest freedom. It is a completely self-sufficient conscious medium.

There is no longer the notion of a "self" walking on this tree-lined walkway. Instead, there is a conscious, awakened, perceiving being that is immersed in consciousness' harmony, peace, and bliss.

In this body that walks while enjoying harmony, fraternity, grace, and beauty, exists the transparent and spontaneous being. There is no "who." It is the being that remains in the here and now, vibrating from its awakened state.

We remain in our awakened being and the consciousness of the Divine Mother emerges.

There is not the slightest influence of the notion of our "self." The being unfolds according to its nature in consciousness. And, there, it resonates in some conscious reality of which it is made, in the planes of the level of consciousness where the Divine Mother reigns. It flows in some reality of consciousness where its being originates.

They are planes of consciousness that overflow with harmony and grace; they lack nothing, nor do they have anything left over. They are realities that exist uninterruptedly in their equilibrium, in their perfection. They are complete realities, they are integral, they are full of existence. They are the levels of existence of the Divine Being, from which the totality of the reality of consciousness is constructed. Within the subtlety of that conscious reality is the force that sustains, procures, and provides in each of the forms, functions, and patterns of consciousness.

These are the realities of the Divine Being that are found beyond the forms of consciousness. They are the conscious worlds that perfectly remain in a unified reality.

For the being that has emerged in one of these conscious realities, they are so concrete that, at that moment, they are all that exists. They develop, overflowing with the pure consciousness that gives the being its existence. The being is coupled with this reality, to which the Divine Mother has given it access. As it emerges, the being discovers that it is an extension of some reality of consciousness of the Divine Being, so it keeps unfolding, stable, firm, and unperturbed in the harmony, grace and abundance of this consciousness.

The dynamism of consciousness is pure beauty. It flows with the precision and in the harmony of its conscious existence. The awakened being delights in adhering to a conscious reality that was always part of it, but which, because of its novelty, it finds to be a new face of its existence.

What we see, what happens, what we witness—everything—is accompanied by the Wisdom of the Being that procures everything with its care, that sustains everything with its love, in the reality of consciousness. That consciousness of which our being is composed and which we experience partially from the mind of our "self."

Everything happens in the conscious environment of the Divine Mother. She patiently waits—beyond the level of consciousness of the mind of each person—for the pathways to open up through which, sooner or later, her consciousness will emerge through the awakened being. Its consciousness is the means for progress, for the formation of our being—the Being that, at the level of consciousness, allows every possibility.

It is all part of a process that happens in the fabric of pure consciousness, in which the Mother of Consciousness exists—the consciousness of the Cosmic Divine in which our being originates.

However, who is it that is experiencing this harmony, this wisdom? Is there anyone there?

It is not a person who is there. In that space within our physical body where the unfolding in the consciousness of being takes place, there is no person. It is only the being that exists and unfolds in the subtle reality of consciousness. Our awakened being enters into consonance with one of the levels of consciousness of the cosmic Being, which provides everything, every possibility, and procures everything, harmonizes everything, sustains everything with its grace, wisdom, and peace.

Our eyes, our gaze, and our awakened being become the window through which we catch a glimpse of the consciousness of the Divine Mother.

CHAPTER 6

The Orchestrator of Emotional Reality

In the labyrinth of the mind, the self and the consciousness of the presence intertwine, forming a complex dance of thoughts and perceptions. The mind often becomes entangled in the illusions of the material world, interpreting each moment through the lens of physical reality. Yet behind these conceptual veils, a silent witness persists: an alert attention that exists free of any meaning. In this introspective journey, we will explore the interconnection between the mind, the presence, and the inner being, discovering the invisible threads that link our daily existence with the deepest essence of our being.

Our mind, in its incessant search for meaning, has never ceased to be the presence that coexists with the consciousness of the inner being, where the divine spark resides. In this intricate weaving of thoughts and perceptions, the consciousness of the being is intertwined with the mind that constantly develops images and scenarios, whether of the past, the present, or the imagined future. The essence of who we are lies in consciousness, but we get lost in the web of mundane interpretations, depending on the material world to give meaning to our existence when, in reality, all we require already exists within ourselves.

Each moment is woven with the meanings, impulses, and judgments of our subjective mind. Yet, behind this frenetic activity, there persists the imperturbability and alert attention of the witness part of our mind, which lives free of meanings and judgments. We create moments with the nuances of our understanding, occupying the inseparable components of the presence and inner being. In this constant creation, the components of the being, in the presence and the inner being, fade into conceptual understanding which, in turn, engages our emotional mood, generating the illusion of the "self."

The being, confused in the search for its sense of existence and certainty in material reality, falls into illusion. The components of consciousness in our mind never cease to be an extension of the pure state of the Presence and inner being in our subtle body. The mind, although it sometimes strays in the search for material reality, never becomes anything close to that reality. Its components are always an extension of the Presence and the inner being, which are essentially consciousness—the same consciousness of which the awakened being, who enters into the reality of the cosmic Divine Beings, is made.

Your mind carries, in its existence, an inseparable link with the awakened being that originates when its components merge in the Presence and in the spark of the Divine within the subtle body inside you.

Unravelling the Dramatic Perception.

In the journey of understanding ourselves, we find the imperative need to purify the mind, an essential process to glimpse the signs of the witness that detaches from tumultuous thoughts and points of view. This inner journey guides us toward the understanding of a being that remains attentive in stillness and silence, observing how the complex notion of our "self" is being generated.

It is necessary to purify our mind so there would be signs of the witness consciousness that detaches itself from thoughts and points of view. This process helps us to understand that there is a being that remains attentive in stillness and silence, observing how the notion of our "self" is being generated.

During this exploration, we become aware of those crucial moments in which a fraction of our mind yearns to enter the level of consciousness where subjectivity is gestated, and dramas are created with vivid scenes of our "self." The configuration of consciousness in the intelligent-emotional realm, where this notion of "self" arises, is not only dedicated to weaving past and future points of view, thoughts, or scenarios, but also stands as a tireless creator of emotional realities.

In this way, the realm of emotional intelligence functions as an orchestrator of psychic reality. This realm of emotional intelligence, in its orchestrating function, has at its disposal the capacity to shape our perception.

As we move forward, we discover that part of our person that resonates with authenticity, tranquility, and balance: an authenticity that connects more with the perspective of the being. From this genuine look at our person, we inquire, discover, and clarify ourselves, consolidating the momentum of the perspective of the being in our mind.

That emancipated, creative, and original part of our being finds special satisfaction while interacting in environments that are free from the idiosyncratic concepts of society. It is enthusiastic about the diversity of the forms and forces of the elements that come into play in spaces, corners, or environments where the hand of man has not interfered.

The gaze that enters the passage which leads to the influence of the consciousness of the being within the mind is absorbed and interacts naturally in that harmony.

In that absorbed, trusting, and optimistic gaze, the influence of the consciousness of the being is revealed. Acceptance, humility, surrender, and silent attention of the presence flow naturally. The awareness of the presence brings an emancipated gaze from concepts that label reality according to utilities, ends, or objectives.

By giving priority to lived experience, in order to directly discover reality, we free our mind from the intermediaries of concepts, allowing immersion in existence in the here and now.

That simple, pure, and innocent being constitutes our truth. Authenticity dispenses with complicated ideologies and fanaticism. The Presence, in its maximum expression, finds its best ally in that authentic, spontaneous, and innocent version of our personality.

In the stripped-down identity of roles and dramas, our presence embraces the adept who is ready to dive into the exploration of consciousness, the very essence of our mind. The welcome of our presence extends to the docile, innocent, and humble identity, a kindred part that ceases to base its value on ideas, expectations, and the feeling of the collective.

In exploring the mind and its intricate relationship with reality, we dive into the complexity of the emotional veil, a component that dictates a pattern of reality to the consciousness of our being, thus creating dramatic points of view. This journey leads us to examine how, even in seemingly unconscious states, such as sleep, this emotionally charged veil lies as an orchestrator of realities, woven together with the facets of intelligence and the subconscious.

The emotional veil—that dictator of perspectives—sculpts a particular panorama in the consciousness of our being, generating dramatic points of view that differ from the conscious existence of the presence. The presence, in its development in mindfulness, does not involve our emotional mood in dramatic elaborations.

The dramatic point of view that emerges while we dream can intensify when we allow ourselves to become emotionally charged. In exploring the dream state, we are faced with the skillful orchestrator of our emotional reality which, in association with the intelligence facet, constructs scenes as vivid as those of any cinematic genre.

During sleep, our mind becomes the orchestrator's blank canvas, where the facet of emotional intelligence and the subconscious collaborate to give life to an illusory reality. While we dream, our mind is at the disposal of the expert orchestrator of emotional reality. In our dreams, the illusory reality arises, which builds the bonding factor that makes up the facets of emotional intelligence and the subconscious. In the dream state, the notion of a subjective entity emerges, revealing our mind's unique ability to create internal narratives, even without conscious intervention.

In the dream, there will always be a point of view that is accompanied by a feeling or emotion. Thanks to this, the notion that there is a subjective entity is established.

It is evident that the perspective of the dream, where this subjective entity is forged, obscures the state of our presence, which resides in a reality beyond conceptual constructs. The subjective entity, fed by the meanings accumulated in conceptual memory, is detached from the reality in which our mind exists—that reality of full attention, freed from meanings and impulses.

The perspective in which there is a subjective entity generated by the subconscious when dreaming eliminates the state in which our presence exists. The subjective entity that the subconscious generates, by taking the meanings of the conceptual experience accumulated in our memory, differentiates itself from the reality in which our mind exists, unfolding in full attention and free of any meaning and impulse. The subjective entity is detached from the reality of the presence.

Since there is a point of view that persists in every instant of the dream, reality is always presented from a subjective perspective. This point of view generates the illusion of a subjective entity. This characteristic prevails independently of the participation of the point of view in the action.

On the contrary, in the waking state, the notion of our "self" finds its focus in the present, thanks to our presence. However, even while awake, a residue of the emotionally charged configuration of consciousness persists, carried by the vital energy and the subconscious.

This residue, a remnant of the emotional charge, contributes to the generation of the dramatic reality of the notion of our "self" while we are awake, a phenomenon that constantly unfolds in the background of our consciousness, often without our conscious awareness. In this continuous play between dreaming and waking, the influence of the emotionally charged veil manifests itself, shaping the way we experience and perceive our own existence.

In the journey of mental self-exploration, we immerse ourselves in the constant practice of prolonging our attention in silence, detaching ourselves from concepts, points of view, and stimuli that cross our mind. This process reveals a gradual transformation by removing the veil of emotional charge that has traditionally enveloped our consciousness, a veil that conditions our mind to follow an intelligent-emotional format that has been established since childhood.

The constant repetition of the practice of mindfulness allows us to glimpse, albeit briefly, the presence in its state of stillness and silence. This glimpse marks the beginning of the shedding of the superficial veil of emotional baggage that has conditioned our mind from an early age, influencing its daily experience.

Our mind has become accustomed to the fact that, even if only briefly, a glimpse of the presence emerges, in its stillness, in its silence, and in the attention that prolongs itself free of meanings and of the stimuli of the emotional veil. We have eliminated the veil of emotional charge that covered our mind and inhibited its perception in the subtlety of the consciousness of which it is made.

This superficial veil is what makes all the difference. When this veil exists, our mind is conditioned to follow the same emotional intelligence format in which, from a very early age, it has been recording its daily experiences. The perspective of the realm of emotional intelligence carries this layer of emotional charge with which our mind omits the reality of consciousness, the reality of which it is composed.

And it omits it because this veil keeps it circulating in its accumulated experience, so it's always out of sync to one degree or another, in relation to the present instant. That is to say, the present instant in which our mind exists in full attention, free of meanings and impulses of the vital energy: the witness position. Apart from being out of sync with the present instant, the emotional charge gives it a slightly coarser sensitivity, which prevents it from perceiving the subtlety of the consciousness of which it is made.

With purification, we have stripped our mind of the emotional veil which, at the same time, has caused it to omit the subtlety of the consciousness of which it is made and of the instant in which it exists in a perfect present. The thoughts that circulate in our mind occur along with a vital energy that is imperceptible, but that is out of sync with the element of the presence existing in consciousness, which is its essence.

Through purification in contemplation, our being acquires from our presence the most authentic humility, equanimity, and surrender.

Purification in contemplation has bestowed upon our being an authentic humility, equanimity, and surrender. As we return to our daily activities, we resonate with the part of our mind where the presence intertwines with the being, knowing that it now enjoys a position closer to the synergy of both. This rebirth invites us to exercise our authentic identity, valuing goodwill and originality in our unique experience of life.

Gradually, the perspective of our self becomes more permeable, opening to the pathways of the level of consciousness of the inner being which, in deep meditation, emerges attracted by the portion of the Divine in our subtle body. The return to daily life is experienced with a rejuvenated self, regenerated and aligned with the present, and imbued with the equanimity of the presence.

This metamorphosis translates into a mind enriched by the conscious nature of our wise presence, becoming its perfect complement. Now, our mind can inhabit clarity, sobriety, and spontaneity in the here and now. This inner journey leads us to discover a renewed and more authentic version of ourselves.

Challenging the Determination of the Unconscious

In the journey towards self-knowledge, the process of shedding roles and dramas reveals itself as a transition towards authenticity. This fragment immerses us in the liberation of the subjective constructs that distort the present moment, allowing us to explore the clarity that arises from recognizing the relativity and incongruity of the character we used to be.

Authenticity becomes a beacon that illuminates the conscious reality of our being, beyond the understandings learned and recreated over the years.

In freeing ourselves from the roles and dramas that weave a veil over the present, we experience a significant transformation. This process involves a conscious letting go: an act of liberation that allows us to rediscover the authentic part of our person. This authenticity manifests itself in the ability to perceive clarity—a clarity that reveals the relativity and inconsistency of what we previously considered certain.

The recognition that our presence exists in a conscious reality of its own, independent of the understandings acquired since childhood, reveals itself as a crucial milestone. This deep understanding invites us to question the mental constructs we have woven over the years, which have outlined our perception of reality.

The notion of "self," once deeply intertwined with subjective roles and constructs, fades to give way to a clearer understanding of the true conscious reality of our being. This reality exists beyond the layers of accumulated knowledge, and connecting with it allows us to inhabit the here and now with renewed presence.

In the process, we emerge as lucid observers of our own transformation. The certainty we experience in our present self contrasts with the faded reflection of who we were. This inner journey toward authenticity and conscious understanding becomes a constant exploration, challenging ingrained notions and allowing us to embrace a more essential and true reality.

In the exploration of mind and the presence, the crucial question arises: how can a seemingly insignificant veil of

The Orchestrator of Emotional Reality

emotional charge exert such a strong power, preventing the presence and awareness of our being from fully entering the reality of consciousness? This excerpt takes us through a journey of contemplation, a process aimed at unraveling and freeing our essence from the layers that conceal it.

The inquiry begins by questioning the nature of that seemingly tenuous but significant veil that dictates the notion of self to our being. In the act of contemplation, we commit ourselves to loosening that veil, to remove the barrier that prevents the presence and awareness from fully entering into the consciousness that composes them.

This veil, which is referred to as the emotional charge, is unraveled in contemplation. As we free ourselves from its bonds, the impulses disappear that induce the mind to overlook the subtlety of the consciousness of which it is made. The stimulus of this emotional layer, although imperceptible, influences the mind, leading it to omit its existence in the present—the space that is free of meanings.

The stillness and silence of attention reveal themselves as essential tools in this process. Here, in this autonomous state of attention, the mind can shed the charge of the vital and immerse itself in the essence of consciousness, free of worldly interpretations.

It is crucial to note that this emotional veil is not only out of sync with the present mind, but it also affects the sensitivity with which we perceive the subtlety of the consciousness of the presence. However, the good news is that all the elements that make up our thoughts, views, emotions, and desires are within this same veiled level of consciousness.

By adopting the witness position, observing and detaching ourselves from mental contents, we allow the presence to emerge. Although it is not yet the pure state, this witness consciousness originates in the Presence, and by adopting it, our mind follows the path that leads it back to its essence.

The more we prolong the witness position, the more we facilitate the emergence of the awareness of the presence. We are, in this way, allowing our mind to penetrate into subtler levels of consciousness that are closer to the pure existence of the presence. This journey into the authenticity and essence of our being becomes a dance between mindfulness and the release of the veils that obscure our true conscious nature.

The Attitude of the Witness - Detachment in daily life

Next, let us discuss the importance of bringing the purifying practice of contemplation into the daily realm. It emphasizes the need to observe and disengage from the construct of the egoic self, fostering the witness position to maintain attention in the present. Throughout the day, conditions are prepared for more effective meditation.

It is essential that, before we engage in deep meditation practice, our mind has already acquired the influence of the inherent aspects of the presence, such as equanimity, detachment, imperturbability, indifference, acceptance and, of course, the ability to prolong alert attention, free of meaning and impulses.

If we prepare ourselves conscientiously, in the intense and constant practice of contemplation, when the time comes for our deep meditation session, it will be dictated by the natural range inherent in the witness consciousness, which has already received the influence of the presence.

In the first instance, deep meditation is a state of consciousness into which the mind enters by having prolonged the witness position in its imperturbability and in its alert attention long enough to enter into consonance with perception in the meaningless mindfulness of the presence.

The dexterous part, adept at deep meditation, is the part of our mind that has already been imbued with the aspects of the presence by exercising the witness position.

And how do we exercise the witness part of our mind? We incorporate the purifying practice into our life. We make it part of our lifestyle.

At the stage of purifying practice in contemplation, it becomes crucial that, during our daily activities, we are attentive to the mind's identification with the constructs of the egoic self. Adopting our spontaneous and transparent identity, flowing in the present while performing tasks, allows the mind to approach the witness position, contributing what is necessary in each moment.

The reflection of the dedication with which we disassociate ourselves from the egoic entity in daily life is manifested in the perception of the presence during our contemplation or meditation sessions. Taking advantage of the time in daily occupations becomes a valuable opportunity to purify the functioning of the egoic entity, which tends to construct dramatic mental scenarios that affect our emotional mood.

Paying attention to mental activity in daily activities creates the conditions for equanimity, silence, and imperturbability of the witness consciousness—characteristics that are prolonged when in contemplation or deep meditation. This prepares the ground for bringing to the meditation session a witness who is willing to follow the Presence in its wise dynamism and silent attention.

As we deactivate the activity of the egoic entity in its dramatic mental constructs, the witness brings us back to the present, keeping our emotional mood intact. This practice frees us from putting conditions on our worth and esteem via external factors.

The mind, by prolonging silent attention, rewards us with a good disposition, automatically overcoming the orchestrator of mood reality, displacing its continuous elaboration of dramatic realities.

The transparency and spontaneity of an identity that flows in the present helps to keep the mind free of speculative activities that generate the notion of "self." Our transparent identity deactivates the functioning of the orchestrator of the emotional and mood reality, i.e. the egoic entity.

In short, progress in meditation is linked to the dedication to stay in a version of ourselves that flows in the here and now, without being distracted by the speculative activity that generates the notion of "self." This constant practice paves the way for effective progress in meditation sessions.

Surrender and Aspiration to the Will of the Divine Being

Let's explore meditation and the connection between the presence, the inner being, and the spark of the Divine. Let's see how the witness part of our mind becomes a channel to allow the emergence of conscious perception, bringing us to a pure state of the Presence and connection with the Divine.

The mind, through its components of consciousness, possesses an innate capacity to adopt the position of prolonged silent attention, thus facilitating entry into meditative states. By adopting the witness position, we allow the mind to make contact with the presence, which remains unbiased in the face of the subjective contents that pass through the mind.

Deep meditation reveals itself as a process where the mind surrenders to the development of its attention, freeing itself from meanings and anchoring itself in the present. This witness position, when prolonged, emits equanimity, stillness, and silence, immersing perception in the subtle plane of consciousness.

The emergence of the pure state of the Presence reveals its aspect of equanimity, blurring subjectivity and allowing the mind to enter into an existence of uninterrupted consciousness, free of meanings and existing in a perfect present.

The Presence, together with the inner being, constitutes the main components of our original self, establishing an inseparable link with the continuous development of consciousness, transcending space and time.

Meditation takes us beyond our "self," allowing the interaction of the components of the presence and inner being with the spark of the Divine. This interaction takes place in an act of surrender, submission, and aspiration to the Will of the Divine Being: the most gracious and truthful being.

The union of the presence and the spark of the Divine in our subtle body becomes a calling, for in that merged state the origin of the Being is found that provides love and wisdom in the reality of consciousness: the mother of consciousness, the Divine Mother.

By adopting the witness position, meditation focuses on concentration within our body, specifically at the level of the heart. Prolonging this position creates the conditions for the presence to reveal a tiny spark, a little light, which indicates an irreversible fusion.

In this process, the subjective mind fades, giving way to an intense aspiration to love, arising from the closeness of the presence to the portion of the Divine. Our being, in the subtlety of this medium of consciousness within the physical body, moves toward the fusion of the presence and the divine spark.

The presence and the inner being are about to become a merged state where consciousness, the Divine Mother, originates, revealing a deeper and transcendental reality of our being.

Being Attached to the Mother of Consciousness

Our physical body, with the marvel that is the nervous system, in which an infinity of neural connections occur in every instant, has always been ready for us to purify and cleanse the emotional veil of the subjective mind to which it is coupled.

Having experienced a spiritual awakening, the change of perspective, existence, and reality is remarkable, but for the intricate nervous system and that field where there are constant neural connections, it is just another configuration of consciousness with which it will now carry its synergy.

The configuration prior to the spiritual awakening was the configuration of the consciousness whose place was in the midst of the presence, as it coexisted with the inner being. The consciousness of the being was offered as the medium of the intelligent, emotional, sensitive, vital, and subconscious facets in which a veil of emotional charge is created. The subtle substance of consciousness that was in our mind was covered with this emotional veil charge, which made it circulate in the accumulated experience.

However, after a spiritual awakening, it becomes the fusion of the presence and wise energy, which links everything, procures everything, sustains everything, and which is every possibility of form and function in the reality of consciousness. In other words, a configuration of consciousness that maintains and develops in its conscious reality without being out of sync with the present moment.

The conscious reality of the awakened being differs from the subjective interpretation of the mind. However, in the configuration of the subjective mind, the same components of the presence, the divine portion in which the awakened being exists, and the subtle planes of consciousness always coexist, without being fused.

There is no conceptual reality that resembles it. It is completely experiential. Nor does it correspond to any of the emotional realities that the subjective mind creates at any given moment. It is a conscious reality, possessing a configuration of consciousness that has not yet reached the subjective mind.

There is an awakened being that operates from the configuration of a consciousness that is free from the notions of the sociocultural and worldly self in which the subjective perspective conceives reality.

As it emerges more and more in its pure state, the being's configuration of consciousness becomes impervious to the influence of existing patterns, conditioning, and impulses of the vital and subconscious.

This influence of the emotional veil charge comes in the form of impulses that are almost imperceptible and that cause our mind to generate a subjective notion, instead of entering into equanimity, where it no longer differs from the instant in which it exists within itself simply as consciousness.

For this reason, we must be aware that the realm of emotional intelligence in which the notion of our "self" is generated carries a veil of emotional charge that has, at the subconscious level, its equivalent in existing patterns and conditioning that circulate through our mind almost imperceptibly, in the form of impulses.

The human mind is determined by what its subconscious dictates. But this awakened being breaks the facet in which the mind is forged under the influence of vital energy and the programming of the subconscious. When the awakened being emerges, the instruments of the subconscious become inoperative.

Under the influence of this awakened being, we explore our daily lives. At the consciousness level of our mind, there is a new player: the awakened being. If we remain in the presence, it carries us in its balance.

When the awakened being emerges, its existence occurs in the development within the conscious medium that gives its configuration of consciousness. It is free of the emotional veil to which it adhered in the intelligent, vital emotional, and subconscious facet with which it omitted its existence in the consciousness that is its very essence.

This configuration of consciousness no longer circulates within the vital charge that, besides being out of sync with the present moment, suppresses the sensitivity in which we perceive in the subtle plane of consciousness of which our being is composed.

When the awakened being is brought to the forefront, it no longer adheres to the veil of emotional charge in which are hidden—but latent—the patterns, conditioning, notions, and stimuli of the vital and the subconscious in which the notion of our "self" was generated.

CHAPTER 7

The Shift of the Subjective Mind - From the Unaware Self to the Awakened Being

On the journey along the path of contemplation, we have experienced a purification of our mind. This process has paved the way towards a deeper perception of our existence. An existence that is more in line with the presence of the being.

While in contemplation, we have already purified enough of our emotional charge to allow it to emanate, even if it is only a glimpse of the perception of the presence that makes us live closer to the present of the being.

On the level of consciousness, our mind has taken on the sensitivity to perceive more closely the subtlety of the consciousness of which it is made. It has acquired more of its equanimity, and this allows it to be more serene in acceptance and contentment. It has lowered the frequency with which our mind elaborates on the dramatic reality in which it engages its soul disposition. The intensity with which our mind reacts to its subjective reality has also decreased.

The Shift of the Subjective Mind

With the purification of the mind and the emerging aspects of the presence, our perception of the world moves away from the rigidity of mundane notions. Now, we will analyze how our mind, influenced by vital energy, constantly interprets and elaborates on its reality and deviates from the pure essence of consciousness.

While contemplating, in the position of the witness, in the prolonging of attention and silence, we encounter this impulse of vital energy that exerts its influence, creating the notion in which our mind differs from its reality in consciousness.

The impulse that carries this vital energy is also the cause of our mind not correctly perceiving the subtlety of the consciousness that comprises it.

The subtlety of the existence on the plane of consciousness, as well concentrated full attention, free of concepts and impulses, are aspects of the Presence.

The vital charge of the field of emotional intelligence is a superficial veil with which our mind obscures the reality of the consciousness of which it is made. The level of consciousness that carries the vital energy that comprises part of our mind is what prevents us from perceiving the details in the subtlety of the presence.

Thus, in purifying the mind of this vital charge, the aspects of the reality of the presence will simultaneously emerge.

All aspects of the presence will emerge simultaneously. That is, its equanimity, its humility, its surrender to consciousness, its imperturbability, its indifference, its full attention, its stillness and silence, as well as its perception of the subtle plane of consciousness.

Without considering this function, with which our mind is constantly interpreting the moment and creating points of view and thoughts, there remains the notion that gives us this vital energy. Of course, we must not forget its equivalent in the subconscious so that, in each instant, our mind omits its existence from the reality of consciousness and replaces it with a notion linked to the mundane human species to which we belong.

The vital energy with which our mind is covered gives it a mundane notion. At the same time, however, it gives it a somewhat coarser perception with which it omits the subtlety of the Consciousness of the Presence. Although the human mind is not as strongly determined by this vital energy and its equivalent in the subconscious as in other animal species, we still carry with us a veil of emotional charge that modifies our perception. This subtle veil influences our patterns, conditioning, and interpretations, guiding us toward what we consider relevant and meaningful, or familiar, among other things.

Thus, in the complex interplay of mind and consciousness, in both animals and humans, there are impulses and patterns that determine our perceptions and reactions. Below, through the observation of a cat and its instinct with regard to a mouse, we explore the depth of these mechanisms and how they affect us in our understanding of the world around us.

The Shift of the Subjective Mind

Let's imagine the mind of a cat sitting placidly, calmly and with its eyes half-open. What happens when it notices a mouse passing close enough to become its prey?

Is there a part of the cat's mind that could make it indifferent to this mouse, which has the potential to be caught at once?

Although we might think that the cat's mind, being in a state of repose, would be indifferent to the mouse, in reality, it becomes something significant and stimulating for the feline's mind. Despite its apparent calm, the cat's mind is loaded with existing patterns, conditioning and desires that encourage it not to miss the opportunity to make the mouse its prey.

If the presence of the cat's mind were to emerge from the state of equanimity, it could be completely indifferent to the mouse passing in front of it. But the reality is that, for the cat's mind, the mouse passing in front of it is significant: it has relevance, it stimulates the cat, and it incites the cat to act.

Even in the apparent calm in which the cat rests, the configuration of the highly charged consciousness of the existing patterns, its conditioning, and the impulses with which this animal's mind is programmed condition it not to miss this opportunity to make the mouse its prey.

Thus, if the cat's mind did not omit its existence in the presence, it would be unfolding in stillness and silence, free from stimuli and the meanings by which it recognizes that the mouse is within its reach as prey. The cat's mind would have been completely stripped of the subconscious instrumentation that conditions it to give it its feline perspective.

Nevertheless, the impulse of its subconscious, which gives it the instrumentality of its survival, persists and programs the cat to act as if it were an automaton. The configuration of its mind is still highly charged with the subconscious that conditions its response in the different situations that present themselves to it.

The impulse of vital energy leads the cat's mind to exert its influence at the instant when, in the reality of its presence, it originally exists only as consciousness.

Likewise, the impulse of vital energy, patterns and conditioning that are its equivalent in the subconscious, lead the cat's mind to exert its influence at the moment when in the reality of its presence it originally exists only as consciousness. It creates a subjective entity that differs from the existence in the here and now that passes only in silent attention.

If we consider that the consciousness of the presence emerged in the mind of this cat, it would be sharing the same present moment with the mouse. The present in which the presence exists, in the here and now, free of stimuli, impulses, desires and meanings. The emergence of the cat's presence would not omit the instant in which its mind exists and unfolds in the concentration of consciousness.

Now, the truth is that the human mind no longer lives with the same vehemence, the same intensity, with this same vital energy and its equivalence in the subconscious as in the minds of other animal species.

However, our mind carries the superficial veil of a vital charge which, in its equivalent in the subconscious, carries existing patterns, conditioning, and impulses—albeit more subtle—that guide it to indicate what is relevant, meaningful, or familiar, among other things.

These existing conditionings and patterns, taken together, form the instrumentation to which our mind, like that of our ancient human ancestors, resorts to generate a mundane human notion of our being.

Without taking into account socio-cultural conceptions, the idiosyncratic concept of our "self," this emotional charge carried by our mind gives it a mundane notion. That is to say, it programs our mind, as it did with our ancient human ancestors, to tell it what needs to be taken into account.

Therefore, the mundane-sociocultural notion that is generated by the functioning that is imposed by the veil of vital charge causes our mind to be out of phase with the instant in the here and now—that here and now in which the subtlety of the presence of which it is composed exists.

In other words, the vital energy gives it a mundane notion and, at the same time, prevents our mind from perceiving the subtlety of its consciousness.

On the other hand, the veil of emotional charge with which it is covered has a perfect match in the intelligent facet of our mind. Both form the realm of emotional intelligence from which we create points of view, thoughts, concepts, and impressions, as well as all the subjective content that passes through our mind.

They generate in our mind the perspective of a subjective entity that we conceive as our "self" and that exerts its influence upon every moment in relation to the environment that surrounds us and the world where we exist.

The subjective entity that is generated from the realm of emotional intelligence recognizes, on the physical plane of matter, what is relevant and significant to it.

When we witness something in the place where we are, it leads our mind to recognize this as the only reality we can perceive on the physical plane of matter. For this, it starts with our body and the other objects that surround us in the environment and, thus, omits in our mind the instant in which its presence exists, in stillness and silence unfolding in alert attention and free of meanings.

Even when we are not aware of it, this vital energy impulse persists and exerts its influence on the level of consciousness in our mind, thereby imposing its peculiar perspective on our presence.

Therefore, the emotional charge causes the original perception of the presence to become the configuration of consciousness in which thoughts, concepts, points of view or any other subjective content in our mind come into being.

The mind recognizes the forms it looks at and, in turn, confers upon them a meaning, a value, and a sense. Its impulse leads it to find something meaningful in the instant—an impulse with which it overlooks its existence in the consciousness that unfolds free of meaning. The subjectivity that arises with this impulse, which moves almost imperceptibly, convinces our mind and indicates to it what is relevant or significant, based on its perspective.

The original state of our mind passes in perfect silence; it is extremely attentive and lives only in the present. It is within the silence—which is prolonged without being misaligned with the present—that the subtle reality of the consciousness unfolds. However, the impulse of vital energy leads the mind to differentiate itself from its consciousness. And, supported by the intelligence facet, it searches for something that has a meaning, a reason, a utility, or an end in the environment of the external reality that it's witnessing.

In contemplation, this impulse of vital energy is almost imperceptible. And we aren't aware of its existence because it has always encased the consciousness of our mind. It is only when we can contrast it with the subtlety of the perception of the presence that we discover the layer of this vital energy that encases our mind.

Contemplation-Unveiling the Subtlety of the Being

After understanding the complexity of the vital impulse in our mind and how it shapes our perceptions, it's important to reflect on how we can purify and dismantle these impulses. Meditation and contemplation are powerful tools in this process. In this way, by unraveling our intrinsic connection with vital energy, we realize the possibility of attaining a state of pure consciousness, free from the distortions imposed by our conditioning. It is here that we immerse ourselves in the contemplative and purifying practice that seeks to free the mind from self-imposed restrictions.

The purification we undertake in contemplation is so effective because, as we become detached from the concepts that travel through the mind, the impulse of the vital energy also diminishes—the impulse that leads our mind to generate the subjective notion.

But why is it this simple to allow the consciousness of the presence to emanate?

Because the part of our mind that pays attention in silence comes from the presence that we want to free from being busy and to become the realm of emotional intelligence.

Thus, when we purify our mind, what we do is observe, one by one—from the position of the witness—the points of view, thoughts, concepts, impressions, or any other subjective content, from the moment it arises until it vanishes in its passage through our mind.

With this, we make the presence detach itself from believing that its existence is the configuration of consciousness in which the thoughts, points of view, etc, that are attached to the emotional charge of the mind pass through.

In this way, we find ourselves in another part of our mind—a part that only pays attention in silence and follows, one by one, the thoughts that pass through to make it clear that we are the witness part of our mind, the one who observes.

However, it is not yet the presence in its pure state that has emerged. As we prolong the position of the witness (in which we pay attention in silence and detach from each and every thought, view, or concept) we allow more and more presence to emanate from our mind.

By purifying itself, the mind acquires, step by step, a new sensitivity to the subtlety of the consciousness of which it is made.

Thanks to this, we gradually release the pure element of consciousness that is embodied in our mind. In fact, once sufficient presence has emerged, our mind takes on the nature of the subtle reality in which it exists.

It is important to mention that these aspects of the Presence emerge together. That is, perception in the subtlety of consciousness, mindfulness, reality in the present moment, surrender, humility, acceptance, equanimity, imperturbability, indifference, stillness, and silence all emerge simultaneously.

This is because all these aspects are part of the same reality of the Presence.

But the equanimity of witness consciousness is the aspect with which we can contrast the impulse that generates this notion in our mind and that makes it distinct from its existence in the subtle reality of the Presence.

When sufficient presence emerges, we can find equanimity. Thanks to this, there no longer exists in our mind the impulse that seeks to exert its influence on the instant that elapses in its original consciousness.

Our mind possesses enough equanimity and it ceases to differentiate itself from the instant, in full attention to itself, which flows free of meaning and impulse in a perfect present.

In fact, there is equanimity because enough presence has emerged of our mind, so that the vital charge stops making it believe that something must be found to give meaning, purpose, reason, or even utility to the present moment.

Nevertheless, we do not cease to perceive. We can open our eyes and what we see is completely imbued with the stillness and silence of the instant that passes, free of meaning. It is the moment of sobriety, indifference, imperturbability, and detachment. We see the objects of material reality only as a background. The equanimity of witness consciousness is more relevant, since the presence has been released for it to remain coupled to its conscious reality.

In this way, it has achieved sufficient equanimity for our mind to accept and surrender to the stillness and silence of its existence in consciousness. There is no element in the external reality that differentiates our mind from being coupled to the development of the subtle reality of the consciousness of which it is made. Hence, those impulses that have been passing through our mind and that are almost imperceptible will cease. That is to say, those impulses in which the mind found something meaningful, something to orient itself with, something relevant in the material objects of the environment that surrounds us will disappear.

With this, we are already within the process in which the functioning of the subjective mind recognizes is deactivated. We are about to blur the perspective with which the being becomes different from its own consciousness. We are precisely at the moment in which the mind intends, with a stimulus, to exert its influence on the original state in the consciousness of our presence.

Simultaneously, when the witness consciousness detaches from the points of view, concepts, or notions that pass through our mind, it also releases the presence from the emotional charge of vital energy.

Now, the element of pure consciousness in the mind is free to be aware of itself. The presence unfolds in the subtlety of its consciousness.

How could the presence emerge without perceiving the subtlety of the consciousness of which it is made?

It can do this because sufficient awareness of the presence has emerged to be able to perceive in the subtlety of consciousness. Thanks to this, we can differentiate between, on the one hand, the clarity, stillness, and alert attention of our witness, and on the other hand, our witness in perfect silence observing the impulse that seeks to interrupt the development of its own alert attention, free of notions and meanings.

The notion of the "self" seeks, in each moment, to give its experience a meaning, to find a purpose, a reason, a utility, an end—or even to take advantage of the instant that, originally in the presence, flows free of meanings.

We rush to grasp meaning in external reality, and what happens is that we interrupt the conscious reality that is the essence of our mind.

Almost on autopilot, the mind brings from its understanding a concept with which it interrupts the natural development in the silence of consciousness. The meaning we derive from reality replaces the development of the presence in the subtle reality of its consciousness. The consciousness of the presence is occupied and transformed by the interpretation we make in the instant.

But can we accept our mind without using it to make an interpretation? Can we be humble and accept its silence without making it interpret something from the lens of our own understanding? Can we let our mind be what it is and allow it to feel the subtlety of its conscious reality?

Yes, this is our being, a conscious entity that exists and perceives independently of what is anticipated to indicate what is relevant, what is meaningful and what is familiar to it at any given moment.

Let our mind taste the present; that present is the conscious reality that is closest to the consciousness of our being.

As we observe the moments in which our mind pretends to replace that stillness—the silence that is prolonged in harmony, peace, and acceptance—we are reestablishing the state of the presence.

This is the reality in which the consciousness our mind is made of exists. It is a state of consciousness that continues unfolding in harmony, in balance, and in attention that passes without meanings, concepts, or points of view.

And the mind, which intrudes and hastens to bring something of its own understanding, transforms the original state of our being. It uses the consciousness of being as soon as it finds something it can interpret with the understanding that it has gradually acquired through its experience and that is engraved in its memory. It uses the medium of consciousness where the presence that converges with the inner being resides.

The concept of our "self" is like a sculptor who always carves the instant to give it a form, that instant that is free of any meaning and flows in silence only as consciousness.

The notion of our "self" rushes to capture with its meanings the present moment that passes through our mind in stillness and silence. We allow our mind to "be" and not serve the concept of our "self". We let the existence of our mind "be."

The Presence Discovers the Divine spark.

After this profound process of introspection and detachment, in which we are confronted with the understanding of our mind and its tendency to interpret and search for meaning, we are at a critical point in our spiritual journey. We are at a crossroads where we have gained some clarity, but we are still on the threshold of a full spiritual awakening. We are now entering the next stage of this journey, that prepares ourselves for deep meditation.

At this point, the consciousness of the being has advanced in its quest to decipher the notion of our "self." But the spiritual awakening in deep meditation has not yet occurred. That is, the state in which our true self lives the reality of the awakened being in a concrete manner and in all its splendor—the splendor in which the cosmic Divine Being exists on the higher planes of consciousness.

Our mind has accelerated the process in which the consciousness of the inner being exerts its influence to reestablish its conscious reality by seeking to transcend the notion of our "self" with more impetus. The purification we carry in contemplation allows the mind to settle into its clarity, peace, authenticity, and truth.

Likewise, the movement in which the presence seeks to transcend the concept of our "self" is intensified. The influence of the consciousness of being gains momentum in our mind.

At the level of consciousness, it has accelerated the synergy that is included in the presence and the inner being and makes the necessary arrangements so that, in deep meditation, their union in spiritual awakening comes without the slightest intervention of the notion of our "self."

At all times, arrangements are taking place within our being for its original components in the Presence and Divine spark to unite.

When our awakened being emerges, it knows nothing but harmony, peace, and love. Our inner being is waiting for us right there, behind the mind that thinks it is the notion of our "self."

The reality of consciousness in which the awakened inner being unfolds is the conscious medium that sustains our existence. Throughout our life trajectory, there has always existed in our mind an interaction between the presence and the consciousness of the inner being and this is forged in the notion of our "self".

Having explored the depths of the presence behind our notions, we move towards a spiritual awakening. In this space, meditation guides us, beyond simple perceptions, directly to the heart of our true essence.

In deep meditation, by remaining detached from each of our thoughts and quieting our mind, the surrender of the witness consciousness emerges and, at the same time, we aspire to be only the Will of the Divine Being.

In deep meditation, when we manage to disengage from our thoughts and silence the mind, a profound act of surrender of the presence occurs. In that same moment, we surrender fully to the Will of the Divine Being. As the notion of our "self" fades, our being, in perfect humility, surrenders and seeks the Will of the Divine Mother.

As the notion of our "self" fades away, our being in perfect humility surrenders and aspires to the Will of the kindest, most benevolent, most loving, and most truthful being at the level of our heart in the subtle body within us. We surrender to the Divine Will absorbed in the concentration of the witness consciousness that is focused within the center of the chest, in the interior of our body.

This is the state of greatest humility and surrender. It is the surrender of the pure Presence of our being that is free to unfold in its level of consciousness. Now, we have surrendered, and there is no one exercising any desire; there are no thoughts and no concepts, there is no persona. The Presence is free to be and interact according to its conscious nature. There is not the slightest notion that pretends to give meaning, interpret, or recognize something subjective in the unfolding of subtle reality that is free of meaning. Perception is no longer that of our identity; it has already been left behind. Now, it is only the being in the development of consciousness in the present instant.

Once the notion of our person has been blurred and is in perfect surrender through our unconditional concession to the Will of the Divine, our presence perceives the Divine spark in the subtle body.

At the level of consciousness, everything remains surrendered, there is no subjectivity that prevents the freely interacting of the Presence and Divine spark from unfolding according to their nature in pure consciousness.

If we allow the witness part of our mind to concentrate its consciousness at the level of the heart, in the middle of the chest near the spine, by allowing the perception of the presence to emerge, we are necessarily penetrating the subtlety of our inner being, where the Divine spark is housed.

There, one develops the absorption of the presence in the concentration of consciousness with an intense feeling in one, or a combination, of love, grace, delight, peace, certainty, glory, or ecstasy of the Divine Consciousness in the moment just before the awakening of the Divine spark.

The Presence discovers the spark of the Divine. The fusion occurs between the Presence and the Divine spark that we have always carried within us.

This is the path of self-transcendence and conscious awakening, where the inner being and the physical body come together in harmonious synergy allowing the consciousness of the Divine Mother to flow through us.

The Awakened Being brought to the Front

The awakened being discovers that its origin is an inseparable extension of the plane of consciousness, where the cosmic Divine Being dwells. The consciousness component of the awakened being, the result of the fusion between the presence and the spark of the Divine within the physical body, correlates with one of the levels of consciousness where the Divine Being resides. This change in the configuration of consciousness replaces the old subjective perspective, where the notion of the "self" was created with a new consciousness that is self-sustaining.

Within this physical body, there is a space where there is only consciousness. It is a space in which the being exists in one of the conscious planes of the cosmic Mother.

This being resonates with the consciousness of the Being that provides and nourishes everything so that conscious realities exist.

The awakened being was brought to the front unfolding in the cosmic reality to which the Divine Mother has given access. There is no longer a person. Now, the consciousness of the being emanates and spontaneously surrenders to the unfolding of consciousness. This is its nature. This is its reality. It lacks nothing. In that unfolding space, its existence overflows.

All of conscious reality develops there, in that instant. In the subtlety of that consciousness, the awakened being enters into a reality that is full of existence, truthfulness, certainty, and grace.

This is how the consciousness of our being exists when the awakened being emanates. It does not require the perspective of a mind seeking wonderful or grandiose things to interpret it.

The awakened being who has emerged, carried by the Divine Mother in its meditations, has become imbued with their conscious reality. In this way, it possesses a wide range of the levels of consciousness in which she dwells.

When the awakened being emerges, in perfect humility and surrender, it enters the superpaths of pure consciousness. It is in consonance with the existence of the Divine Mother. It is trying out the reality of the Being that reigns in the reality of consciousness.

The mind, which, in its tireless creation of subjective realities, sought the value, confidence, and esteem of the person, is replaced by an experience free of concepts, which overflows with existence.

And this is not surprising because, even before spiritual awakening occurred, even before we undertook an intentional purifying practice, the components of the presence and inner being were always present. And these, although not merged, correspond to the same plane of consciousness of the awakened being and the reality of the Divine Mother.

This being is self-sustaining within the conscious environment of its existence. There, it finds everything it needs. It has ceased to look for anything other than development in the consciousness of its origin, of its essence.

In fact, its origin in consciousness exists in a unified reality brimming with existence that continues to develop in the balance of its harmony, peace, and delight.

The awakened being emerges in one of the planes of consciousness to which the Divine Mother gives access. It unfolds in a conscious reality in which it is coupled, on the subtle plane, with the Divine Being that continues to sustain and make possible the totality of the reality of consciousness. In this way, the awakened being emerges to discover that its origin is an inseparable extension of the plane of consciousness in which the cosmic Divine Being abides.

The consciousness component of the awakened being—a product of the fusion of the presence and spark of the Divine—corresponds to one of the levels of consciousness in which the Divine Being exists.

The presence and inner being, even when they are not fused, have always been the conscious medium in which the notion of our "self" is generated. This is the consciousness that has been adjudicating the notion of our "self" to make us believe its existence is separate from the being. The subjective perspective of our person has been occupying the consciousness of the being and has made it believe that the reality that concerns it is that of this perishable physical body.

However, the conscious medium of being has always been part of our mind. Our mind has always been sustained, even before spiritual awakening, by the components of the presence and consciousness of the inner being that carries the Divine spark.

Our mind—that which gives us the notion of our "self"—is largely formed by the components that, fused together, evolve in the planes of consciousness where the Divine Being dwells.

It is a triumph that, in this physical body, within the same nervous system where an infinite number of neural connections take place in every instant, the mind that has used the components of the presence and inner being to create and recreate the notion of a "self" takes over.

In other words, it is a change of state. But what was coupled before and after the spiritual awakening were components of cosmic consciousness. Cosmic consciousness that was entangled with concepts in the realm of emotional intelligence in which the notion of our person was generated and functioned.

The shift from the subjective mind to the awakened being is that of moving from a state of consciousness that generates the notion of a sociocultural "self" to that of a Cosmic Being.

Always, it was the cosmic consciousness that was coupled with the incessant neural connections as the subjective mind or as an awakened being.

The love of the awakened being emerges in the same conscious medium that is connected to the infinity of neural connections in its incessant activity within our physical body. The mind, which used to generate only the notion of the "self," has changed its configuration. Now, it is the fusion of the presence and the Divine spark that is included in the inner being within our physical body.

The Presence, merged with the Divine spark, has transcended the notion of our "self." The consciousness of that awakened being has been taken to test the consciousness of the reality in which the Divine Mother exists.

The wonder of the nervous system, with its incessant neural activity is fulfilling its purpose of carrying the consciousness of the Divine Being that gave it its design and its function.

In fact, in the complexity of the nervous system and in the intricate nervous system and in the constant neural activity, there was always a mind that carried, even without being fused, the cosmic elements of consciousness as the Presence and the inner being.

Everything works great; they are perfect for each other. Mission accomplished.

The physical body and the awakened being function in unison, cooperate in synchronicity, and serve as instruments to the consciousness of the Divine Mother.

The consciousness of the Divine Mother finds a standing collaborator that walks from their perspective in some spot of this sacred planet—an emancipated space that follows the laws of its nature in the cosmic consciousness of the Divine Mother.

A glimmer of consciousness has opened up at the origin of their existence.

Our awakened being serves to establish, in the medium of consciousness, the spiritual experience of the physical body that is also part of its design.

The Shift of the Subjective Mind

How could the synergy of an awakened inner being that emerges and develops in the conscious reality in which it is composed and the physical body that serves as its vehicle occur, unless they are both part of the same Divine plan?

Before and after the spiritual awakening, our mind always serves the cosmic Divine Beings—whether the components of the presence and the divine spark are fused and give rise to the awakened being, or whether they coexist to generate the notion of our "self." In both cases, they are extensions of the pure Cosmic Beings that remain and exist, uninterrupted in their conscious reality.

Although they are not fused, the presence and the inner being coexist and, together, they seek to transcend the notion of our "self."

The consciousness components of both presence and inner being that our mind carries are waiting for us to allow their union. They are ready to take the leap to experience the conscious reality of which they are made.

The human mind, in all its activity, in its imagination, in its creativity, in its aspiration, in its yearnings and in its motivations, conceals the being that seeks to transcend the notion of the "self," in order to return to the origin and cease to be only an extension that differs from the pure state of its essence. The consciousness of the being in our mind seeks to return to the source, to the Mother of consciousness.

And, in this search to transcend the notion of the "self," the drama of life takes place with which, at the level of consciousness, paths are opened that will serve to connect to the presence and the divine spark that we carry in our inner being during deep meditation.

Body and mind meet at this stage of life to achieve the transcendence with which the evolution of the awakened being begins.

Behind the mind of this person, who was busy and preoccupied with their beliefs, preferences, and convictions, there were always the components of the presence and inner being—components that, even without being fused together, coexisted and influenced each other. They have opened the way for a fertile conscious environment for spiritual awakening.

Now, if we pay attention to any part of this physical body, we feel the flow of consciousness circulating unceasingly in the hands and fingers, or inside the head or rib cage.

We did not know it, but in our physical body, everything has always been ready to accommodate this being that is now awake.

Now, we understand that the totality of this physical body is an organism that is designed to fulfill the function of serving as the vehicle of the awakened being.

CHAPTER 8

Reality in Consonance with Being

The mind, which believes itself and takes the "self" very seriously, carries with it a subtler reality of consciousness: the consciousness of its original being. In the mind of the person, this manifests as their goodwill and is reflected in the nobility of their aspirations, motivations, and intentions. It is revealed in the gaze that is immersed in the present moment, unfolding in harmony, in the grace of beauty, and in delight. It is found in the attentive perception that flows in silence, surrendered to the present moment and unburdened by thoughts.

Contemplation becomes the path to this state of consciousness: a space where our mind finds its true soul disposition, without depending on external circumstances. Here, in the tranquility of the present, the notion of our "self" dissolves, allowing the mind to rest in its own conscious nature.

Immersing ourselves in serenity, calmness, and balance of mind is so simple that sometimes all it takes is to sit and witness a fragment of nature. We forget about the dramas of our daily lives, the stories told by our persona and seen in the media and the news, and events that constantly engage us and shape our reality. We immerse ourselves in a state of optimism and peace, without the need to analyze why we feel so complete, calm, and satisfied. In those moments, nothing is missing; there is only serenity and optimism.

It's like a moment when we are walking on a beach, enjoying the sensation of our feet being caressed by the waves. In that moment, our mind does not interrupt our good mood by reminding us of the events in the morning news.

It so happens that, precisely when we are immersed in the enjoyment of the moment, we don't even realize it. It just happens. This is because it is the most natural state of our mind. It is the reality of its conscious nature. It is a moment of spontaneity and innocence. At that moment, our mind is not busy paying attention to the role of our persona.

If the mind serves any purpose in its subjective functioning, it is to create the notion of a person through intelligence, feeling, and emotions.

We create images in which we substitute the present instant by giving it meaning and value, making judgments, suppositions, conjectures, predictions, entertaining suspicions—and involving, to different degrees, our feelings and moods.

From a conceptual perspective, we develop images of past, present, or future events. These scenarios, which we build with images, are of our own creation.

Although these subjective images are very similar to the reality that flows unperturbed and indifferent in a continuous present, when we interpret them, we resort to the conceptual understanding that comes from our past experiences, which causes the mind to detach from the present instant, from the here and now.

For example, when things in our work environment are not going well, our mind often goes into a state of anxiety, dissatisfaction, and vulnerability. There is a combination of emotions and mental processes, where the emotional part is mixed with the intellectual part, giving rise to expectations, judgments, conjectures, assumptions, speculations, and suspicions, among others. Most of the time, the activity of our subjective mind occurs within this emotional-intellectual framework.

This configuration of the realm of emotional intelligence takes over the consciousness of our being and exploits it in its interpretative activity. It does not rest; everything it grasps affects it. Everything it recognizes through meanings, concepts, and points of view, accumulated from our experience, becomes part of its present reality. It does not miss the opportunity to interpret the situation, embellishing with something of its own creation. It does not matter whether it agrees or disagrees with ideas, beliefs, values, preferences, or opinions; it always recognizes meanings, on which it bases its reality at that moment.

If there is one thing that this realm of emotional intelligence in our minds is engaged in, it is creating and recreating an idiosyncratic and mundane conception of reality. Like every individual who is part of society, we register ideas, customs, expectations, values, and feelings from the configuration of the consciousness of this realm of emotional intelligence in our minds. The experience stored in memory is not just conceptual or rational content; it is always accompanied by an emotional dimension. It contains the feeling of what is acceptable or unacceptable, beneficial or detrimental, valuable or insignificant—both for us and for the group to which we belong: our community, society, etc.

It is true, however, that this realm of emotional intelligence is inseparable from the consciousness of being; otherwise, it would not exist. It requires the conscious medium provided by the being to become a reality in the present. It is evident that our thoughts are not the same as the being's presence, but they contain a part of its presence, which gives them existence in the present. While our thoughts occur in a partial present, which is the subjective reality we elaborate on, in our mind there is also a perfect present, the present of the presence. It is the present of pure consciousness, which cannot cease to exist in an uninterrupted and conscious manner.

The subjective functioning of the mind uses the conscious medium of the presence to perceive reality according to what it considers significant and relevant in the present instant. The notion of our "self" intermingles with events and situations from the notional conception involving our emotions. This reality may seem compelling, as it causes us anxiety and makes us feel fragile and vulnerable, among other emotions. However, at the level of consciousness, it's as simple as this: the presence that coexists with the inner being is used to transit through the accumulated emotional charge and takes shape according to our constructed subjective images, concepts, and scenarios.

At the level of consciousness in our mind, these are simply fluctuations from one configuration of consciousness to another—from one configuration that is closer to the conscious nature of the presence and inner being, to another that does not cease to circulate within the emotional charge that has accumulated in the memory, bringing with it meanings that will develop a subjective reality.

Emotions and accumulated vital charges feed the perspective of our "self," creating an illusion that turns us into partakers of all that encompasses the conceptual understanding of the mind. Both events take place in the conscious medium, composed of the presence that converges with the inner being, coupled with the infinity of neural connections in the nervous system of our physical body.

Therefore, we're going to rehearse this journey in which our mind reconnects with its good emotional disposition while we prolong our attention in silence, freeing it from thoughts and meanings. Our mind does not necessarily need to translate its emotional disposition into the concepts it uses to construct the reality in which it exists. The present of the consciousness of the being is more related to peace and harmony than to interpretation, assessment, judgments, conjectures, guesses, assumptions, or any speculations we may make in the moment. If the consciousness of the being and its present are more linked to the best of our emotional disposition in the moments where we're interested, immersed, and optimistic—that is, in the here and now—why allow them to fade away in events that are far away from our life? We forget the inherent capacity of our mind to enjoy itself, and to experience happiness and optimism.

In those moments we enjoy—while either alone or accompanied, delighting in the sea breeze and feeling that we are part of the immensity of this planet as we contemplate the celestial sphere—we are in the here and now, in the present of our authentic, spontaneous, and carefree version of ourselves.

Likewise, when in contemplation, the reality of the peace and harmony of the being emanates naturally from our mind. We do not need the external factors that make a moment pleasurable, pleasant, or enjoyable for our mind to be imbued with the consciousness from which its good mood originates. We do not need those conditions in which our mind understands that it can enjoy and be fulfilled. We lay to rest the concept of our "self" and, thus, it does not intervene with its speculative activity.

The Harmony of Being

In contemplation, we allow our being, in all its fullness, its certainty, and its joy, to emanate from our mind. We make peace with our existence. We accept ourselves and love ourselves, as we did in the best moments of our youth or childhood. That same clear, innocent, carefree, spontaneous, and transparent consciousness is also found in the mind that is carried by the adult. That state of clarity, peace, and harmony is already in our mind. It does not matter that, when we look in the mirror, we see an adult who, with the passing of life, has been fragmenting that certainty, tranquillity, and fullness within their mind.

We shed the character, the concept, of our "self." Although there is a physical body, there is no notion of a person. This is the occasion when we allow the mind to be without our "self."

We let go of the concept of our "self." We release its influence. We allow equanimity to emerge in the silence, in the attention that is free of the meaning of our witness part of our mind. We do not expect anything from the silence, stillness, and subtlety of the emerging perception. We exist in the here and now.

We accept the initial state of how we experience our "self." We accept it, so we can be aware that this state in which we perceive ourselves is ready to transform and allow the witness consciousness to emerge in its full clarity and subtlety. We accept this field, which we have taken for granted and in which our mind is vibrating, which has become the standard or normality of how we experience ourselves.

Best of all is that everything is happening while we are detached from the thoughts that pass through our mind. Our mind has the option of participating, or not, in the thoughts that pass through it. If we simply pay attention in silence, without identifying ourselves with those thoughts that pass through, we are opening the pathways through which the consciousness of the presence can emerge. In doing so, we detach ourselves by observing them, one at a time, from the moment they arise until they fade away.

The witnessing mind's detachment, in the prolonging of attention in silence, allows us to perceive things from a subtler, clearer awareness. What we are doing is taking the presence of our being out of the configuration of consciousness in which it has been perceiving itself. We obtain a consciousness that is closer to that of the being, and which enjoys existence in certainty and satisfaction, carefree but without any condition that merits it. It is serenity, calmness, and enjoyment that needs nothing aside from being. It is not conditioned to anything. It is just part of us. It is part of our self.

Not only do we detach ourselves from thoughts, but it also becomes clear to us that our inner witnessing mind is there, paying attention, immovable and imperturbable. It remains immovable because it persists in stillness and silence, and imperturbable because it no longer assumes the thoughts are its own reality. It no longer surrenders to the thoughts as they pass by; it simply observes them, from the moment they arise until they fade away.

We do not bring meanings; we only allow the presence to emanate in the silence that is prolonged, while we are in "witness" mode. In those moments, it is the witness part of our mind that remains indifferent to the thoughts, concepts, or notions that pass by. We allow ourselves to feel how the being recovers its natural state in clarity, in alert attention, and in the subtlety of its existence, free from the meanings of the mind.

We let go of the part of our mind that seeks to exert its influence. Now it is only our being as witness consciousness that remains in the unfolding of the instant that is free of meaning and impulse. It is the being that experiences all that happens in the stillness and silence of our consciousness. We are exploring from the perspective of the being, which exists in transparency, innocence, and spontaneity.

The interpretation, which we create with meanings from our accumulated experience, yields and gives way to the being that exists only in the instant, in the here and now of consciousness.

As we progress, our mind regains its presence and immerses itself in balance, serenity, and the glorious present moment. We free our mind from the emotional complexity that has confused it, replacing the experience based on emotional turbulence with a clear and serene understanding.

We purify our mind to regain the connection with its center. Our mind resumes its present in balance, in serenity, in the here and now. The notion of our "self" intrudes on the events, bringing its own conception, involving our emotions.

We strip it of the tangle of the emotional charge that confuses it, and we substitute it with existence in the equilibrium of its center, with an understanding that is fed by harmful emotions.

As we intensify this purification and acquire more and more of the reality of being, the incongruity of the mental scenarios in which we involve our feelings—which we previously believed to be our concern—will become more obvious. We move closer to the reality of our being. So, if our mind continues to participate in the reality of media, social networks, and the multitude of discourses that circulate here and there, that other part of our mind will notice.

During all this time, we have been purifying our mind and, thanks to the constancy of our contemplative practice, we have purified it of a good part of the emotional charge. In reality, what seemed to be an insurmountable structure of subjectivity in our mind was only a superficial veil of vital charges.

That veil of superficial emotional charge has the effect of deceiving the presence. It leads it to omit perception in the subtlety of the consciousness of which the mind is made. And, at the same time, this veil of emotional energy has the effect of throwing the mind out of alignment with the present instant, in which the consciousness it is composed of exists, thus causing the mind to circulate again and again within its accumulated experience.

As the presence emerges, we also purify the mind of what obstructs its contact with its good emotional disposition. At the level of consciousness, this emotional disposition in serenity, harmony, and peace originates in the Divine spark of the inner being.

We do not need to be in a special place, nor do we need to imagine anything to reach this level of consciousness. Everything happens within the silence of our mind, without thoughts. Thanks to this, we allow a good mental disposition to emerge, together with this silence that has been prolonged in attention.

We purify our mind and, therefore, as it emanates more and more consciousness of the presence, it escapes from the emotional charge that has kept it alienated—that is to say, actively isolated, developing subjective reality and involving in it its feelings, its emotional part.

The illusion that is generated by the expansive movement of conceptual understanding, which involves our emotional disposition, becomes evident.

We will test if, by purifying the mental charge while in contemplation, this optimistic mental disposition emanates together with the silent attention in the enjoyment, immersed in the subtlety of its own existence.

There is already a part in the concept of our "self" that is aligning itself to serve in the process that is engraved in the consciousness of which our being is made.

The components of the presence and inner being, although they were not previously united, have always been in our mind.

Through a purifying process, in which we have acquired the ability to detach ourselves from the concepts and meanings that circulate in the mind and to remain in prolonged silence, we have managed to open the doors to harmony, peace, and certainty. These are all aspects of the consciousness of the inner being, which at its core carries the spark of the Divine.

The Link with the Subtle Plane of Consciousness

Once we have incorporated contemplative practice into our life, by experiencing just a hint of perception on the subtle plane of our presence, we have the key to initiate ourselves into spiritual practice.

When the mind of the spiritual practitioner is accustomed to experiencing hints of the perception of their presence, their mind acquires a sensitivity on the subtle plane of consciousness.

Having created the habit of prolonging the position of the witness, who detaches themself from the activity of their mind in their equanimity, imperturbability, stillness, and silence, we are ready to allow, through deep meditation, the pure consciousness component of our mind to enter into its natural link with the subtle plane of consciousness.

Perception on the subtle plane and alert attention are inherent aspects of the component of the presence in our mind. It is precisely because of this sensitivity of having acquired the perception of our presence that, in deep meditation, the spiritual practitioner in perfect surrender and aspiration for the Will of the Divine Mother alone to be done, unveils on the subtle plane of consciousness where the spark of the Divine exists in our inner being.

At the beginning of our deep meditation session, we need to focus the concentration of our consciousness at the heart level, in the middle of the chest, inside our physical body and in the direction of our spine, in surrender, in which we give ourself up to the Will of the most kind, most truthful, most loving being and place our existence in their hands.

It is fundamental to understand that, as this glimpse of pure consciousness emerges, it is no longer a partial or fragmented state of consciousness. Rather, it is the same Being that remains uninterruptedly unfolding within consciousness and which constitutes the cosmic Presence. The same cosmic Presence in which the Mother of consciousness exists. The Divine Mother.

That glimpse of our presence operates in the same continuous, uninterrupted reality on one of the planes of consciousness where the Being exists in which consciousness originates.

With just a glimpse of the perception of the Presence in its pure state, we are accessing within—in our subtle body—the reality of consciousness that is an inseparable part and design of the Cosmic Divine Being. Pure consciousness emanates, revealing the conscious reality in which the Divine Being exists uninterruptedly, transcending time and space.

The inseparable link we carry to the Divine Being is unveiled; it emanates, blossoms, and now comes to the forefront of consciousness so that, in this moment, the laws and the reality in which our being lies are indistinguishable from any of the realities in which the Divine Mother exists.

What is happening is that the being, as it emerges, takes its existence in the Cosmic Divine Being in which it originates and with which it has never lost its connection or link. This awakened being is no longer in a partial state, as it was when there was only the coexistence of the presence and inner being in the subjective mind. The essence of the awakened being is now the fusion of the presence and the spark of the Divine we carry in our inner subtle body. This being is governed by the laws of the nature of consciousness and not by the existing concepts, conditioning, and patterns that give the subjective mind its mundane and idiosyncratic notions.

Embracing the Reality of Consciousness

The being that has fully emerged is automatically, naturally, and spontaneously linked to the reality in which the consciousness originates. The full states of the awakened being are perfectly integrated into one of the realities in which the being that procures all exists: the being that sustains all, that gives all possibility, and that is the origin of consciousness—that is, the Divine Mother.

In the cosmic consciousness of the eternal Divine Mother, this dual aspect of the Presence and inner being exists in an inseparable state, fused and unfolding in the higher levels of consciousness. This is why, if we allow them to enter the interaction they are called to perform by their nature in consciousness, the presence part that resides in our mind automatically seeks union with the other spark of the Divine that resides in the inner being, which gives way to spiritual awakening.

The awakened being emanates in the fullness of its existence. In this state of existence, we enjoy our freedom of being, navigating through the web of consciousness that surrounds us. We are exploring the subtle reality of consciousness, transcending the level of the subjective mind. Our being prefers the subtlety and harmony of its own conscious reality; this is its ideal environment. This conscious reality is where the being within our physical body wishes to reside, the one who has explored in meditation the higher planes where the Cosmic Divine Being resides.

Is there the notion of a "self" that is kept busy, acting out the drama of an identity that is being elaborated, based on ideas, worldview, and in the feeling of the collective?

In the previous stage of our life, our mind did not stop interpreting at every moment by resorting to the meanings stored in our memory, thus generating not only the conception of our "self" and its relationship with the environment, but also conditioning our mood.

By allowing the awakened being to emerge, which arose through the linking of our presence with the spark of the Divine in deep meditation, the soul disposition radiates with its verve, its abundance, its certainty. It is no longer clogged up by the layer of emotional charge it was covered with when it first developed its views.

This vital charge served as food for the subjective mind for the elaboration of its dramatic reality. The automatic response of the notion of our "self" was to seek value, certainty, security, satisfaction, and esteem in external factors or conditions and not in its own harmony, peace, or abundance of the influence of being in our mind.

The emotional charge blocked the ways in which we can be more in tune with the goodwill and nobility that originates in the consciousness of our inner being, creating a feeling of dissatisfaction: that something was missing, not enough.

Is there a "self" that replaces the conscious reality that has emerged from the awakened being?

It understands the motives and reasons of people who feel vulnerable and outraged when they believe that their present consists of the events that are reported in the media, on the internet, or in the protests that take place in the streets.

Will this being that is connected with harmony, peace, the love of its consciousness, replace its present with what the collective feels?

It is not mere romanticism to say that the conscious reality of the being is inseparable from the present moment.

If we can have a notion of the present that we feel in the here and now, it is because the reality of the consciousness of which our mind and the Cosmic Divine Being are made cannot exist but in a perfect present.

The present of the existence of being is not that of the reality of concepts involving the soul disposition of people.

The being, in a perfect present, exists together with the concentration of consciousness and pure existence; one cannot exist without the other. They are all aspects of the same reality in the Presence—the presence of which our mind is largely composed is the same as that which merges with the divine spark in our inner being, or that which is carried by Cosmic Divine Beings, such as the cosmic Presence and the Divine Mother.

As the conscious existence of the being emerges in the same present instant of the fabric of consciousness in which the majesty of the natural scenery is immersed, the images and the feeling of the projection of a person who is doing the experiencing will dissolve. We delight in the existence of the being. There is no "who." There is, however, a being—a being that doesn't differentiate from its existence in the reality of consciousness.

The perception of the being that has emanated is direct. It is coupled with its reality in consciousness. It is the experience of the being that lives without the veil of a subject-object entity conception. The consciousness of the awakened being perceives directly in the conscious medium both in its own essence and in the fabric of consciousness in the natural environment.

Our mind has shed the veil with which it now perceives in the consciousness it is made of; it is returning to its world, to its home. What it carried inscribed in that veil of emotional charge that covers it is what kept it recirculating in the conception it accumulated in its memory.

The inscription of experience from the realm of emotional intelligence inhibits our mind from perceiving the subtlety of the conscious reality of which it is composed.

It is as if, before, our mind would, at all times, wear the costume of an identity that constantly clung to the emotional intelligence format in which it adhered to the vital charge that is accumulated in the memory.

Now that the consciousness of the being is awake, it is enough to remain in the Presence to perceive without the impermeability that omitted and maintained a distance with its own conscious reality.

This is the moment of glory for the Divine Mother. This is her victory: to have in her world, her realm of consciousness, a witness who informs her according to her conscious reality.

The cycle has been completed at the level of consciousness in the mind of this spiritual practitioner.

We go through the purifying process, where we already acquire from our presence its ability to detach from the concepts and meanings that circulate in the mind, in order to remain in prolonged silent attention.

Enjoyment, contentment, harmony, peace, certainty, abundance, joy, exhilaration, and delight are aspects of the consciousness of the inner being that carries the Divine spark at its core.

The subtlety of the consciousness of the being, taken in some of its conscious realities, becomes the most concrete, the most reliable—the one that endures behind the subjective reality that the mind elaborated. This is our being that has been touched by the consciousness of the Mother. It now feels a sense of belonging in the conscious reality of the being that is all kinds, that procures all, that sustains all, and that is behind the totality of the processes in which consciousness is progressing.

At that moment, our existence is united with the reality of consciousness to which the Divine Mother gives us access.

Where did the mind of the person go? What remains is only the conscious platform that does not cease to unfold in the existence of the consciousness of which it is made—the consciousness that we felt made permanent the existence of our "self." Now, the existence resonates with some of the conscious realities of the Divine Mother. Whatever comes from the Divine Mother seduces it, hypnotizes it, is irresistible. Our being becomes docile, obedient, and aspires to caring for the being that procures all, that sustains all, that fills us with grace, certainty, and abundance.

Would we exchange this care for the activity of the mind that sought to satisfy the notion of our "self?" Would we exchange this life experience for the one that spent its time elaborating on scenarios of the past, of what it interpreted as its present, or that predicted some situation of the future?

Does our mind get attached to the political propaganda that is pasted on the wall next to the sidewalk we are walking on? Is there anyone who develops a conception, a few points of view, and involves their soul disposition to replace the instant in which the awakened being unfolds in grace, in harmony, in the here and now?

Of course, we could stop, and begin to develop some points of view that are accompanied by a feeling, but is it necessary? Is it relevant? Are we going to substitute the joy of the existence of what our awakened being brings us? Does what is written in that political propaganda have anything to do with the present in which the consciousness of being unfolds in its harmony, in its peace? Is there the notion of a "self" that becomes a participant of the ideas, and that implicates its feelings in the messages communicated by those papers stuck on the wall?

It would be better to allow the consciousness of being to flow in simplicity, in delight, and in beauty.

We are delighted with the harmony, the peace, and the certainty that the symphony of conscious reality brings us; we enjoy existing in our free being, which is coupled with the Divine Mother, transcending the fabric of consciousness of the environment where we are. It is the subtle reality of consciousness that we are revealing, penetrating behind the level of consciousness of the subjective mind. Our being prefers the subtlety, the harmony, of its own conscious reality. That is its medium. That is the existence that is relevant to it.

That state of consciousness is the one in which the being that goes inside our physical body wants to be. The being that has experienced, in the deep meditation the consciousness of the higher planes in which it exists the Cosmic Divine Being. There is no greater truth or certainty, than the consciousness in that existence.

Our being nourishes itself by feeling harbored in its home, in its consciousness, and in the spiritual fabric that it is in every corner of this sacred planet.

CHAPTER 9

Collective Memory - Transcending the Social Identity

*I*n a world where definitions of identity are intertwined with social expectations and cultural categories, how can we discover the authentic essence that resides beyond these limitations?

Let's explore how spiritual practice and contemplation can offer us a glimpse of the presence that exists independently of thoughts, emotions, and social roles.

How could we have known that our mind's consciousness exists independently of thoughts, views, emotions, and the idiosyncratic, worldly view of our person?

With just a glimpse of the presence, which has always been our mind, we simultaneously shed the idiosyncratic notion of both our "self" and the collective.

We discover there is a being that is separate from the physical body and we learn what it represents in the collective culture, including gender, race, sexual orientation, community membership, and social position, among other categories.

That emancipated part of our person is akin to our wise presence. We have stopped building the concept of our "self" according to the set of ideas, customs, expectations, values, and temperament of the collective that preserves in its memory the imprint of the idiosyncrasy that it has inherited from past generations.

The notion of our "self" is already sufficiently empowered to leave its positioning within the illusion of the collective's memory. That version of ourselves has become adherent to the inquiring, enlightening, and purifying practice of our wise presence.

And later, when in contemplative practice, we experienced the first glimpse of our presence, we understood that the existence of our being in the here and now is free of the concept of the "self" that, in some facet of our life, we constructed based on the roles, characters, ideas, and expectations of the collective.

The path in which the emerging presence dwells is unreachable by the idiosyncratic meanings that are registered in memory. The experience of existence in the stillness and silence in which it abides and unfolds in the subtlety of consciousness has no conceptual equivalent.

Contemplation is the perfect occasion for our mind to let go of the meanings with which it creates its conceptual interpretation at any given moment.

Now, it has emanated a glimpse of the presence in a warrior mind that has already gone through a series of tests through which it has acquired the training to enjoy its new being.

The being behind our mind is determined from a very early age by the programming of the collective memory.

It is part of the design of the Divine, into which the mind of every person enters to record their life experience from the perspective of emotional intelligence. As spiritual practitioners, it is necessary for us to detach ourselves from this idiosyncratic and mundane vision to which we are hopelessly subjected.

The reward is that the presence can emerge with what remains within its reach to unveil the spark of the Divine that we all carry in our inner being.

The idiosyncratic and mundane programming that occurs in the realm of emotional intelligence has its equivalent in a veil that covers the consciousness of our being.

For the spiritual practitioner, this means that, at the moment in which we are contemplating and meditating—as we are detaching ourselves from thoughts, concepts, impressions, or any other content that goes through our mind—at the same time, we are freeing the consciousness of the being from the level of consciousness of that overlay.

All the programming that is registered at the level of consciousness in our mind, plus all we have acquired, along with what our ancestors gained from collective memory, is exposed in the form of thoughts, concepts, impressions, or stimuli that are ready to be disseminated, and to cease to be part of the level of consciousness of our mind at that moment.

It's as simple as that. As we draw out the consciousness of the being in the detachment exercise, we remove from our mind the existing patterns and conditioning we have inherited from the idiosyncrasy and temperament of the collective. The consciousness of the being is re-establishing its conscious nature, which in essence, is part of the Cosmic Being.

The totality of the idiosyncratic and mundane record with which we generate the notion of our "self" is inscribed in a being that is, at root, cosmic consciousness.

We carry an essence of cosmic consciousness that we engage, in every instant, to generate a sociocultural and mundane concept. We carry in our mind the same reality of cosmic Presence that functions and develops in its conscious reality. But, because of the superficial veil of the emotional charge, this cosmic existence becomes the conceptual reality in which we perceive our person and the world in which it dwells.

This emotional charge is what maintains the functioning our mind enters to participate in the realm of emotional intelligence in the collective memory.

And so, as the veils of our conditioned perception begin to lift, we begin a profound transformation at the level of consciousness in our mind. We realize that our consciousness, the very fabric of our mind, exists independently of social constructs, thoughts, emotions, and personal identities. This revelation is an invitation to explore the deeper facets of our being, to recognize a "self" beyond the confines of gender, race, social status, and the myriad labels we have inherited. With each step, we move closer to the presence within. A presence that defies conceptual understanding and invites us to embark on a journey of purification.

The fact that our being is now the instrument of the Divine Being is the best tribute we can pay to all minds. Meaning, all beings that were formed as we were, by creating and recreating the concept of a "self," sustained by the idiosyncrasy and memory of the collective. Each one of the minds that has carried the components of the being in the presence and in the Divine spark in its inner being, goes through this stage in life. A stage in which the pathways are opened so that, sooner or later, its two components of consciousness—the presence and the Divine spark—embark upon their union.

They carry out their union when the consciousness of the being of our mind transcends the notion of our "self." The components of the presence and inner being, with their core in the divine spark from which every human mind is made, have it dictated in their itinerary to bring about this link. Due to their nature in consciousness, the presence and the Divine spark of our inner being are destined to unite.

In our being, we carry, in the presence and the divine spark that is the core of the inner being, the components of the cosmic consciousness. Our mind is made of the same reality in which the awakened being exists, which is coupled in some conscious plane where the Divine Being resides.

In the collective memory, as in our individual memory, the experience with which the conception of what each individual is, as a part of society and the world, is accumulated. This understanding is not only conceptual, but the mind lives it through its emotional part by involving its feelings in the temperament of the collective. This is the area of emotional intelligence in which—both as individuals and as a collective—we create and recreate the conception of ourselves as human beings and of the world. The idiosyncrasy of the collective, its ideas, expectations, and values, are intimately related to a temperament and a feeling. This reality is the collective memory.

The components of the presence and the subtle inner being—which belong, from a very early age, to the same reality as the cosmic consciousness—have been serving as a conscious means for our mind to constantly create and recreate the concept of our "self," based on the conception of the memory of the collective.

Our mind, by taking the configuration of consciousness from the realm of emotional intelligence, creates for itself the conceptual and emotional reality of the collective memory. In this way, it sustains its value, confidence, security, self-esteem, and sense of belonging.

As long as our mind is not purified, no matter how original our perspective may be, if it is conceptual, it necessarily belongs to the same level of consciousness of the emotional intelligence realm, in which the collective memory functions.

The experience of living in the cosmos of consciousness, which also exists here in this world, is a direct experience; it is not conceptual and does not involve the feeling or temperament that is shared with the collective memory.

On our inner journey towards self-discovery, we will explore the powerful resource our mind has to enter the passage that takes us to the origin of the Presence: the witness consciousness.

Witness Consciousness

In our meditation sessions, we bring our skilled witness consciousness, capable of prolonging its awareness in detachment, experiencing perception in the calm, sobriety, in the stillness and silence of our presence.

Thus, we ensure that the transcendental reach of our meditation sessions is marked by having allowed the original component of consciousness to manifest: the presence.

During this time, we will employ the witness part of the mind to free ourselves from identification with the thoughts, moods, impulses, desires and notions that circulate in our mind. This exercise allows our mind to effectively enter a state of deep meditation.

In the position of the witness, we will detach ourselves from the subjective contents of our mind, and thus, emerging from this practice, we will experience prolonged alert attention, free of impulses and meanings. This attention will penetrate the pure component of consciousness that is the presence.

This wise mechanism is simple but powerful: as we prolong the position of the witness, which remains imperturbable and immovable in the face of the thoughts, moods, impulses and desires that pass through our mind, the component of the presence is detached from the intelligent-emotional realm that envelops our mind.

As we intensify and prolong the alert attention of our witness in perfect silence, aspects of the presence, such as equanimity, imperturbability, and indifference, emerge from our mind. In this way, the consciousness of the presence in our mind, leaves its transit in the registers of the intelligent-emotional format of conscious memory.

The nature of the presence remains rooted in the here and now; this allows the mind to no longer be out of phase in its transit through conscious memory, seeking to give meaning to the present moment.

Prolonging the consciousness of the witness, which sustains within equanimity, alert attention, in perfect silence and free of meanings, the notion of our "self" blurs.

This is the moment in which the liberated consciousness perceives itself on the plane of consciousness that transcends the meanings, notions, sense and impulses, which generate the conception of our being separated from its essence.

Everything happens in the same mind that thinks, that gets excited, that feels. We are allowing it to exist in its original level of consciousness, which is the presence.

The presence's perception on the subtle plane of consciousness, has the power to reveal, in the center of the chest, at the level of our heart, within our physical body, the spark of the Divine within our subtle body, with which the evolution of the awakened being begins.

It is evident that the ability of our witness part of our mind to prolong its detachment in alert attention, equanimity, surrender and silence is the key to beginning spiritual practice.

The witnessing mind, upon reaching the perception of pure Presence on the subtle plane of consciousness, finds its best ally in the most authentic aspiration for love and unconditional surrender to the Divine Being. Surrender intensifies and love is enlivened as concentrated attention penetrates the subtle body that houses the Divine spark within our physical body, at the level of the heart, in the middle of the chest and towards the spine.

Directing the concentrated attention of the witness from the beginning, focused on the center of the chest, at the level of our heart, within the physical body, at the moment in which it reaches perception on the subtle plane of consciousness and penetrates into the inner being, also enters into the intensification of unconditional surrender, into the being that is pure love, certainty and goodness, the Divine Being.

At this moment, the notion of our "self" no longer intervenes, and the experience becomes the reality in which the presence and the inner being coexist, which at its core carries this tiny little light that resembles a small spark.

The components of consciousness of our being, the presence and inner being, come into interaction, without the slightest interference from a subjective entity. The presence and the Divine spark are free to carry out their union.

In this space of inner connection, we have allowed the skilled witness to guide during meditation. We have journeyed towards the core of our being, exploring the vastness of our consciousness and discovering the connection with the divinity that resides within us.

When the light of pure consciousness dissolves the shadows of our previous perceptions, we find ourselves facing a new reality, stripped of the layers that once defined our existence. We shed the veil of collective memory and the notion of a limited self. We open ourselves to the vast universe of consciousness, where the true awakened essence resides and waits, ready to illuminate every corner of our existence.

Beyond Collective Identity

By the union of the presence and the spark of the Divine, the perception of the awakened being emerges where the limited "self" fades away. A realm of pure consciousness emerges—a subtle perception that transcends words and thoughts and guides us into the conscious reality of the awakened being. The awakened being unfolds at the origin of its unified consciousness. The being enters the sacred dance of subtle reality where the Divine Mother resides.

This face and this body, which we have seen change over the years, now serve as an instrument for the awakened being, who has coupled with one of the conscious realities of the Divine Mother.

How distant is the influence of the concept of the "self" that lived the reality of the collective.

And our body is there, in the same place where it could be elaborating on the projection of our accompanied person, involving our soul disposition. The harmony, the wisdom of this consciousness, which does not separate itself from the present instant in which its conscious reality exists, becomes unattainable for the vital energy in which the subjective reality is generated.

It is consciousness that is made untouchable by the existing patterns of the subconscious. It is so well positioned in the consciousness to which it was given access by the Divine Mother that it does not fall into the illusion of the subjective entity.

At the level of consciousness, our being could still be in the facet in which it considers views and thoughts (which also involve our emotional part) as an immovable, unquestionable reality. However, it now unfolds and is obedient, held by the hand, surrendered to the reality of consciousness where the Divine Mother has given access—as if it were a stamp, a copy, in that conscious reality in which it flows.

The reality of the concepts that make up its sense does not distract it; this consciousness is immersed and flows in harmony, equilibrium, and the peace of the conscious existence that it has adopted.

This consciousness has everything it needs to keep our being overwhelmed. There, it exists and develops, coupled with the conscious environment to which it belongs.

We are living in the here and now of our awakened being in one of the planes of consciousness of the Divine Mother.

Does the concept of a person exist who assigns meanings while gazing at the everyday life situations of people who live in the same neighborhood? Or is the person gazing from a worldview based on some system of ideas? Or is there somebody interpreting their experience based on concepts about philosophy, art, science, or anything else?

The consciousness of the awakened being is emerging, which, having been imbued with the reality of the Divine Mother, witnesses from the perspective that sustains and keeps everything linked in harmony. That is where each element of reality acquires its rightful value—where all human activity is seen happening in a web of consciousness. The individual mind carries out its actions in a web of consciousness that is sustained by the conscious reality of the Divine Shakti.

The world of the consciousness level in the emotional intelligence realm is perceived from the perspective that is sustained in the awakened being—the being that has already tasted, on several occasions, the splendor of the reality in which the Cosmic Divine Being exists.

We are experiencing the same cosmic consciousness of the Cosmic Divine Being within us.

The awakened being has entered one of the planes of Divine Consciousness. And, although we are in that same place where what predominates is the mantle of the collective consciousness, the awakened being has taken on a configuration of consciousness that is made untouchable by the subconscious.

We can appreciate and remain within the grace of Divine Consciousness, even in a cityscape. To be in the cosmic consciousness of the Divine Mother in this body and to see, in full color, scenes of daily life in our neighborhood, is revealing. It is as if we are looking into the city, the neighborhood, from a glimmer of consciousness that, until now, appeared to be cloaked, covered by the collective consciousness.

The perspective of the awakened being runs behind, parallel to the level of consciousness of the idiosyncrasy and the realm of emotional intelligence that occupies and veils the reality of the presence.

The consciousness of the awakened being possesses the power of grace, beauty, and harmony, and it remains completely emancipated from the notions with which it interprets reality, from the subjective perspective that goes under the influence of the subconscious.

The perception of the awakened being has superseded worldly conception.

Our being enters into consonance with cosmic Presence. It flows in the stillness and silence of consciousness and unfolds in the reality of the Presence.

The perspective of the awakened being, who has sampled the conscious reality of the levels of consciousness where the Divine Mother exists, carries a wide range of realities of her levels of consciousness. This being sometimes experiments with the cosmic Presence and sometimes with the aspects of the Shakti, in grace, delight, beauty, and harmony—and even in Divine ecstasy.

At the level of consciousness, the being that has transcended the notion of our "self" has emerged. The awakened being that is the product of the merger, of the presence and the spark of the Divine within the inner subtle body, returns to the consciousness of the Being that gave it its origin. The Mother of Consciousness. The Divine Mother.

The awakened being, by its nature, seeks to enter into the conscious reality of the Divine Mother—the being that gave it its origin. That conscious existence is its house, its home. There, it joins in the subtle reality of the consciousness of the being that sustains, procures, provides, and allows the functioning and the realities in the realm of consciousness.

There, the awakened being is docile and malleable; it surrenders to adopt the form given to it by the consciousness of the Divine Mother. It rejoices; it is part of the being that gave it its origin. It unfolds in one of the eternal realities of the consciousness of the Divine Mother. It is the awakened being that has accessed one of the realities, aware of the existence of the Divine Mother somewhere in the cosmos of consciousness, on this sacred planet, in which nature, cities, neighborhoods, parks, etc, as well as what is both inside and outside our physical body, are immersed.

We look at the city, and we see its buildings, but the existence of our being is coupled with an existence that is not out of alignment with the instant in which it unfolds in the reality of consciousness in a perfect present.

Everything we witness in that landscape is a background to the harmony, peace, and abundance of the state of consciousness in which the existence of our being unfolds.

The veil, with which our mind obscured the existence of being in the consciousness that is its essence, has vanished. When the being emerges, wherever we are, what is relevant is the instant in which it exists, coupled with the consciousness that gave it its origin.

Whether it is one or another conscious reality, all are complete, all are brimming with existence, and all are in perfect harmony. All are part of the fibers of consciousness from which the Divine Mother plays the silent notes with which she sustains, nurtures, procures, provides, and makes possible everything in the reality of consciousness—in the conscious reality that is the essence in our mind, even before spiritual awakening.

The awakened being, in the truest humility and in the subtlety of that simplicity, is in consonance with one of the higher planes of consciousness of the Divine Mother. It resonates with the supermind that inhabits the higher planes of consciousness.

There is no greater joy than to be a servant of the Divine Mother on this earth!

The fact that our being is the servant of the Divine Mother is inscribed in the nature of consciousness; it is the return of the being to the consciousness of which it was always an inseparable extension.

The consciousness of the awakened being, which has taken on some of the realities of the Divine Mother, was brought to the front. This consciousness takes command of our being and, in its subtlety, flows with an attention that escapes the vital energy of the environment through which we travel. Its reality is impenetrable by any other consciousness than that of the Divine Mother.

It is the queen of conscious realities. In the Divine Peace it exudes certainty; it is imperturbable and remains developing in its domain, on the plane of consciousness.

The consciousness of the Divine Mother carries the wisdom of being the sustainer, the provider, the caregiver in the reality of consciousness.

What a joy that our being is touched by her consciousness!

At that moment, our being takes on the configuration of the symphony of the mother's consciousness, so that, no matter what we see, we can always understand the reality of her reign. The territory of consciousness is her domain. She is the queen.

The consciousness of the Divine Mother exists and remains in the same place where you walk, interpreting and recognizing meanings with which you replace the instant that exists in your mind, in silence, in full attention, free of meanings.

The Divine Mother waits patiently in the facet of your mind where you have created the concept of your "self," based on the idiosyncrasies of society, and on your conception of who you are and the world around you.

Currently, in the lifestyle that many individuals are adopting, the abandonment of ideas, customs, values, and expectations that were based on the idiosyncrasy of the collective is evident.

We are seeing the birth of a new generation of individuals, who are opting for a simple life: one that is in keeping with their authenticity and is independent of the idiosyncrasies of the collective. In addition, these people are abandoning the ideas and habits of the consumerist lifestyles in which the masses participate.

This is a reflection of the transformation that is taking place due to the progress of the being, which—at the level of consciousness, beyond the mind of the person—exerts its influence to remove that which hinders the progress that leads to transcendence.

The being finds an ally in a simpler, humbler, and more authentic version of our person at the level of consciousness—one who can cooperate in the process of deciphering the notion of our "self."

The being, which is an inseparable part of our mind, does not have to deal with the concept of a "self," of an identity, which could be intensely dependent on sustaining its value, self-esteem, and sense of security and belonging through the ideas, customs, expectations, values, and the feeling of the collective.

What is even more important is that this new generation of individuals, because of their independence, live their day-to-day, their reality, and their present almost without sharing their ideas of this idiosyncrasy and without involving their feelings in the temperament of the collective.

The present of these people no longer moves at the dizzying pace in which the person seeks their value and self-esteem in what they recognize, and values idiosyncrasy with that which diminishes speculative activity.

It diminishes the activity of the mind that generates images with which it replaces the instant in the here and now, in the present, making judgments, supposing, conjecturing, predicting, suspecting, and involving to one degree or another its feeling, its soul disposition.

Thanks to the freedom of the being of these individuals—in their originality, in their peculiar way of seeing and doing in life, without conditioning their value, their self-esteem, in what they recognize as the conventions and expectations of the collective—they enjoy existence in a reality that is more aligned with their being.

In the minds of these people, the distance to the consciousness of their true self has been shortened.

The fact that more and more individuals are opting to break with the old structures in which the collective consciousness functions is an indication that the human spirit is emancipating itself from what hinders it in its progress towards transcending the notion of the "self," which has been sustained in the idiosyncrasy.

The influence of the being behind the mind is arranging for the re-establishment of our reality in consciousness to come.

Made in the USA
Las Vegas, NV
15 April 2024

88684201R00111